M000200903

Golf Tough

Practice, Prepare, Perform and Progress

by Dan Abrahams

Published in 2014 by Bennion Kearny Limited.

Copyright © Bennion Kearny Ltd 2014

Dan Abrahams has asserted his right under the Copyright, Designs and Patents Act, 1988 to be identified as the author of this book.

ISBN: 978-1-909125-50-6

All Rights Reserved. No part of this publication may be reproduced, stored in a retrieval system, or transmitted in any form or by any means, electronic, mechanical, photocopying, recording or otherwise, without the prior permission of the publisher.

This book is sold subject to the condition that it shall not, by way of trade or otherwise, be lent, re-sold, hired out or otherwise circulated without the publisher's prior consent in any form of binding or cover other than that it which it is published and without a similar condition including this condition being imposed on the subsequent purchaser.

Bennion Kearny has endeavoured to provide trademark information about all the companies and products mentioned in this book by the appropriate use of capitals. However, Bennion Kearny cannot guarantee the accuracy of this information.

Published by Bennion Kearny Limited
6 Woodside
Churnet View Road
Oakamoor
ST10 3AE

www.BennionKearny.com

Cover image: ©Shutterstock/rangizzz

To David Baillie, Head Professional, and to the
members of Dulwich & Sydenham Hill Golf Club

Fortuna Sequatur

Acknowledgements

I'd firstly like to thank my publisher James for his continued help, guidance and support. Big hugs and kisses to all my family – most notably to Heidi, my wife, who continues to edit my work with intelligence and integrity, and whose love, affection and attention help build the highs and guide me through the lows.

Thanks to all those involved in England Golf – thanks for your warm welcome and thanks for giving me the platform to help others search for greatness.

Thanks to John Franks for his suggestions – by the way, you've made my website rock!

Thanks to the Gray family - in particular to David Gray, who allowed me to write about his father's inspirational story.

A massive thanks to those who have participated in the book – Chris Sells, Rod Gutry, Hugh Marr and Phil Kenyon. You are all inspirational in your own way – thank you for allowing me to share your stories and your wise words with the golfing world.

And perhaps most importantly, thanks to you, the reader. If you get one idea, one technique, one different playing philosophy, or just one tool from this book… then I hope you feel I've done my job. Good luck!

About the Author

Dan Abrahams is Lead Psychologist for England Golf, as well as a former touring professional golfer and PGA golf coach. He has worked with players globally at all levels - from amateur through to tour professional golfers, and he has previously been a lecturer for the British PGA and a county coach in England.

He is a registered psychologist who has a built up a global reputation for his work in sport. His passion is to de-mystify sport psychology for golfers and deliver simple and practical ideas for players to implement on and off the course. He is a regular speaker at coaching and sport psychology conferences across Europe - inspiring audiences with his original, engaging and fun presentations and workshops.

His two previous books – Soccer Tough and Soccer Brain – are international bestsellers. Dan continues to spread his golf psychology messages across the golf globe by using social media. His philosophies are used by players in Europe, America, the Far East, and Australasia.

Dan can be reached on his Golf Twitter account **@AbrahamsGolf** or his Soccer one **@danabrahams77**

About the Contributors

Chris Sells. StrokeAverage.com is the brainchild of founder Chris Sells, who started working as the official golf analyst for the English Golf Union in 2001. Over time Chris's reputation has grown to the point where he is now regarded by peers as a leading contributor to the game of golf, with a full understanding on what it takes to become a great golfer.

StrokeAverage.com is unique in its depth, flexibility, and ease-of-use. It is designed for players and coaches of all standards, from club golfers to Ryder Cup stars, and your local club pro to world renowned golf coaches. The company's client list speaks for itself. StrokeAverage.com consults to leading tour players such as Rory McIlroy, leading golf coaches such as Peter Cowen, and leading golf organizations such as the English Golf Union. To date - whilst working with StrokeAverage - their clients have achieved dozens of tour victories, four Major championships, one PGA Tour Money List and two Race To Dubai victories. Chris can be found at **www.StrokeAverage.com**

Rod Gutry has been a Tour caddy since 1998. He has worked extensively on the European Tour and European Ladies Tour. He teaches golf strategy and course management to all levels of golfer, from amateur through to professional. He can be found at **www.rodgutry.com**

Hugh Marr is one of the UK's leading coaches of elite players, specialising in player development. Hugh works with a number of European and Challenge Tour Professionals, as well as many of the country's leading amateur players, including National and Walker Cup team members. His roles include Lead Boys Coach for England Golf and former Head Coach for Surrey Golf Union (2007, 2008 & 2009 English National Boys Champions). In addition he is a regular contributor to Golf World magazine. Hugh can be contacted at **www.surreygolflab.co.uk**

Phil Kenyon. Phil is Director of Harold Swash Putting Ltd at Formby Hall in Liverpool. He is a PGA professional and a sought after 'specialist putting coach' and has worked with many of the world's leading players. Phil has a Master's degree in Sport Science. His client list is one of the most extensive in world golf and he conducts workshops with governing bodies and associations globally. He can be contacted at **phil@haroldswashputting.co.uk**

Table of Contents

Introduction

We're going to begin with the end in mind.

What you are about to read is your future golfing self. It's a description of you competing under pressure but doing so in a controlled, confident manner. It's you managing your thoughts, dealing with distractions, and expressing the behaviours that help you tune into high performance. It's you playing steely, determined golf; it's about you being Golf Tough.

So sit back and mentally place yourself on the golf course. It can be your home club or it can be the course of your dreams. Now, pick a competition. It can be a medal round you play every month, or it can be a flight of fancy, like the Masters or The Open.

Make the sun shine, throw a hint of breeze into the air, and put yourself on the 18th hole and on the fairway.

Approach shot. You know what is needed - one more solid swing and a couple of putts - three shots to a tournament winning score.

"STOP" – forget the score. Be in the now, be present.

Your brain has an eye on the prize but you know it's important to ignore the grey matter. Being Golf Tough you know that the brain is the great distractor.

You've held it together down this back stretch of holes – don't let your thoughts get the better of you now. Relax! Affirm the positive, just one more solid swing needed. A few deep breaths, get the yardage and settle into your routine.

Left is water, right a deep bunker. "STOP" - cut the negatives quickly. Danger was for the preparation routine, now you're into your performance routine. One-six-five to the flag; six iron. Middle of the green – rifle it straight. You tweaked it left on the last "STOP" – "SHIFT" – forget the last, be now and be present. Just swing smooth and find the middle of the green. Be Golf Tough.

Introduction

It's a nice six iron. Reach for the club and now step into your bubble of excellence. Cue focus, cue confidence, and cue technique. Be Golf Tough.

A couple of practice swings – your blueprint. Create a feeling of incredible confidence – a relaxed swish through impact. Feel a great strike in your mind, that addictive feeling of nothingness through your hands, through your arms, and through your heart. Hear that perfect strike, like a rough scrape along a fresh piece of sandpaper. As you release through impact, and drive into your follow-through, envision the ball stream away. Hear it fizz. See the perfect trajectory, and see the ball land softly next to the pin. Feel it, see it. That's it, your brain's blueprint created. Stand behind and stare down the target.

Now start your walk towards the ball. Not just any walk, a confident walk. Eyes locked onto target, stride perfectly paced. Then into a solid setup. Feel comfortable, feel strong, feel powerful and feel athletic.

A look at the target, then back at the ball. A waggle to release any remaining tension. Then fire! No thought, just do – with a lingering sense of tempo through the ball.

The ball rips through the air. A great strike, and at first straight as an arrow. But a fade starts to appear as the ball gently works left to right. As you watch the flight your physiology begins to go into overdrive – your heart races and your mind shoots thoughts behind your worried eyes. Your brain, that prediction-making machine, fears the worst. For a moment it looks as if a sand shot looms – an up and down required to take the title. But luckily your ball grips and holds the green.

Out of judgement mode, into post-shot routine. Into tall and stride. Label how you feel as you move on – keep that inner voice firm. Tall and stride, tall and stride. Keep managing your physiology as you approach the green. A long two-putt required, confidence must be maintained. Be Golf Tough.

"I've putted well so far don't scr...." "STOP... SHIFT." Manage your voice quickly. Tall and stride, tall and stride.

Believe as you walk onto the putting surface. That sense of commitment. That sense of complete confidence. Read the putt with belief then a couple of confident and evenly-paced practice strokes. Confident and even. Confident and even. 30 feet left to right. Enjoy the freedom in your shoulders and arms but lock your eyes onto the target. Now let it go. Confident and even.

A nice stroke, a nice strike and the ball takes the break. But it rolls three feet past. Your heart sinks slightly. "STOP" – stay in belief, tall and stride. Tall and stride. Momentum of confidence is vital. Keep your inner voice to a minimum. A clear mind is required for this last stroke.

A final putt - three feet of ground to cover. Do so with belief - body to drive mind on this one. Read it with commitment, stride the hole and trust what you see. Pick the target and settle into confident practice strokes. Confident and even. Confident and even. Now place the putter head behind the ball, a look at the target and stroke it. Re-create the blueprint...

...and in! Golf Tough accomplished.

Golf Tough

This is your golfing future. I hope you're excited. It is a world of self awareness and self management. It is a world of self monitoring and self evaluation. And it holds the prospect of shifting your current golf philosophies and uploading a new way of thinking, being, and doing, on the course, on the practice ground and on the putting green.

Reading the narrative above may seem daunting - some new words to add to your golfing vocabulary, some strange phrases and some different ideas. All will become clearer as you work your way through Golf Tough, but this isn't a book for the fainthearted. I'm not going to go easy on you. I'm not going to tell you how great a golfer you are. Nor am I going to promise you that great golf awaits you.

Great golf requires effort and trust and patience. It requires introspection and honesty - the ability to look at your game squarely in the face and decide exactly *what* it is you need to improve to explore the next level. It requires intelligence – emotional, critical thinking, and imagination. It requires practice. And, as you will discover, not the type of practice that most golfers engage in, but individual, specific, comfort zone challenging practice that stretches you to the max.

Stretch is the optimum word here. As a sport psychologist I think of myself as a stretch not a shrink. This book isn't Golf Weak, it's Golf Tough! It's about *you* knowing *you*, the golfer. It's about developing a plan for *real* improvement. It's about having a game face – about taking hold of yourself on the course rather than allowing the elements or other external factors to determine your game, your round, and your score. These are Golf Tough traits and they encompass the journey I want to take you on.

Blunt I may be, but I've long since learned that pulling punches renders you a punch drunk golfer. Most recreational players (and plenty of professional ones too) have no structure to the mental side of their game. They walk from tee to ball and from ball to green as a slave to the conditions, to the environment, to their bad shots, to their score, and to the opposition. They lurch from thought to thought, from feeling to feeling, as inconsistency echoes throughout their game. The fact is - to play your best golf consistently, and to truly discover how good you can really be - you need a mental structure for your game on and off the course. This is what Golf Tough offers you - a template for excellence no matter what your level, no matter what your age or your experience.

Enter my world

So welcome to my world. In my world how you think from shot to shot matters as much as your shoulder turn or your release through impact. In my world the quality of your focus in and around the ball is as important as your ability to move your shots away from danger. In my world managing your mindset is as vital a component of performance as your swing plane.

My world is the psychology of golf. It's thinking, it's feeling, it's focus. It's laying down the right performance processes to help you manage your golfing attitude on and off the course. It's forming the mini behaviours that elicit success under pressure. And it's tracking strengths and weaknesses and building the optimum practice environment to help you become as good as you can be.

It's a world that is more often than not intangible. Whilst mindset manifests itself behaviourally, it can hide itself quietly beneath the surface of swing, tempo and stroke. And while it can be seen through routine, through body language and through commitment of swing, mindset is often ignored or dismissed as unimportant or less impactful than its technical and physical counterparts. We still live in a golfing world of turn, transfer, hinge and release.

This is perhaps as it should be. Golf, after all, is a game of movement. Poor technique, no matter what your mindset, will lead to errant shots and inconsistent scores. Having been a professional golfer myself I know how important technique is. If you can't return the club back to the ball in a consistent manner you will struggle to improve, even if you enjoy a tough mindset and a confident persona.

But I warn against complacency. Don't take mindset for granted. Shots are spilt (as well as some tears) because of a drop in confidence, because of a distracted focus, and because of the burden of emotion. Rounds are destroyed by bad thinking, by the crush of negative self-talk, and by pervasive inner pictures of poor shots that linger. These are just for starters!

The golf mindset can be teasingly simple yet enduringly complex to get right. Do you know how to turn down the volume of distraction? Do you know what to think to enhance your self-belief? Do you know how to practice to improve your performance confidence? Do you know how to re-wire your brain to develop your swing technique quickly and effectively?

If you *do* have all the answers, then do you practice this area of the game? Do you take time, deliberate time, to work on your golfing mindset? I ask this question because there is a gulf between 'knowing' and 'doing'. It's one thing to know what to do; it's another thing to *do it* – in the heat of battle, under pressure, when it counts. You may know the science, but can you apply the art? In golf, it is the brush strokes that mediate success and not the palette itself.

The 4 P's of Golf Tough

I'm going to borrow from my playing days. As a struggling professional golfer roaming the mini tours in Great Britain and Europe I didn't practice with precision. I didn't prepare effectively. I didn't take control of my performances. My progression stilted with every year of experience I clocked. I reckon I graced the tee a worse golfer at 24 than I was at 17 years of age, and largely because of the mindset I approached the game with.

And so I present you with the four sections of Golf Tough: Practice, Prepare, Perform and Progress. These sections hold mindset philosophies and techniques to help you 'know' and to help you to 'do'. This may seem like a personal bias - troubles from my own golf playbook - but I can assure you in a decade of consulting at every level of the game, as well as at the elite level of other sports, I have found that competitors tend to lack the right mental approach in one or more of these four areas. And they offer a neat and concise way of defining the mental game of golf. Let's take each P in turn with a brief description.

Practice

Why practice?

Before answering this seemingly obvious question, stop and think. Take a little time over the answer, it's important. It's important because the *why* of practice drives your practice behaviours. It drives your attitude on the range and pitching area, and it drives your focus as you execute swing and stroke on the chipping and putting green.

To my mind most golfers answer this question incorrectly. Most golfers will claim that they practice to improve - to get better. This formula is only partly complete. Golfers should indeed practice to develop their game. They should practice to develop the skill required to shoot the scores they dream of. But while skill is your entry point to excellence, it won't walk you through the door. I want you to play Golf Tough, which means you need to dedicate yourself to practicing for skill *and* confidence. It is skill encased in a bubble of confidence that holds the keys to high performance under pressure.

Golfers should train to build confidence. They should hit balls to feel more confident with that 180 yard hybrid shot into a small green. They should practice putting to feel confident over a three footer. They should practice pitching to feel confident with 50 yards to the flag. The golfer must strive to develop skill *and* confidence in equal measure - they will unite to produce a pressure-proofed game. They will gel to produce Golf Tough time and again.

Practicing to improve skill and confidence is difficult. It requires focus and patience and perseverance. It also requires intelligence. The 'beat balls' mentality doesn't work. The 'find it in the dirt' grind doesn't work. The mindless motion of ball after ball without thought or imagination doesn't work. In this first section I will help you develop skill *and* confidence.

I will also teach you the *what* and the *how* of practice. There can be no excellence without practice, but unfortunately there may be no excellence *with* practice. The golfer who works hard at her game doesn't always enjoy a smooth trajectory of improvement. You need to be smart about your training.

If you want to develop your game you must firstly know *what* you need to improve. Few players do. Many hit the driving range without a sound knowledge of the strengths and weaknesses of their game. They practice with blinkers on, sometimes blindfolded, often with tunnel vision. They have less impact on their scores come the weekend. To be Golf Tough you need to be a student of *the* game and a student of *your* game. You need knowledge of the underlying numbers that make up your final numbers. Chapter one will unfurl your practice blinkers.

Chapters two and three will teach you *how* to practice. We will explore ways to incorporate confidence training into your sessions – simple processes that are fun, interesting, and which help you to leave the range *knowing* the margins of your golf game and regularly *knowing* that you are a better golfer than before you arrived. I will also introduce you to the important neurological processes that underpin your ability to nurture technique more effectively and subsequently develop skill quicker.

All three chapters in section one are written with skill development, confidence building, and the *what* and *how* of effective practice in mind. They are written to help you find solutions to the most frustrating element of golf – improvement! Making the secrets of game improvement habitual will help you to prepare to play Golf Tough.

Prepare

The first tee is the beginning for most golfers. For me it's the middle.

When you stride onto the first hole, much of the hard work should have been done during your preparation and planning. You should know your course strategy before you park your bag next to the tee – plan A, plan B, complete! You should have much of your performance thinking ingrained – goals set, thinking strategy set!

Effective preparation quietens the mind. It allows excellence to flow. It helps peak your attention at the right time in the right places. It helps you alleviate anxiety and manage pressure, and allows your confidence to soar. There is no room for panic, for worry or doubt, when you have spent a few days covering all bases and encouraged a mindset of certainty. Great thinking in the build-up to a tournament reduces the brain's capacity for destructive negatives – those that sap your energy, reduce your confidence, and bring distractions to the fore.

At the heart of sport psychology lays the concept of *momentum* – a hidden force that sways back and forth as the game develops. We see it in tennis when a player elicits confidence from winning a few points in a row. We see it in soccer, as a team starts to string passes together culminating in wave-after-wave of pressure on their opponents. In golf, momentum scatters birdies or bogies depending on the direction of impetus. Being Golf Tough means being able to build or break momentum accordingly. And that safe time, before you play, is the time to build a momentum of confidence. It's also a time to work out how you will manage a momentum of focus – if it goes wrong, how will you deal with the immediacy of failure?

Section two introduces you to the process of preparing to play Golf Tough. The words you use, the attitude you have, and the behaviours you display leading up to the first tee shot heavily influence the score you sign for at the end of the round. To open this section I am going to help *you* get to know *you,* the golfer. Golfers who have an acute knowledge of their preferred game face find self-management on the course easier and are more flexible with their thinking when adversity strikes.

Next we will explore the optimal way in which to strategise and plot your way around the course. Having a game plan set out before you compete helps you to think less when your mind should be directed towards the simple process of play. Of course the strategies you sketch need to be executed with certainty and with an emphasis on self-management. I will teach you to encase your game plan in a shot routine that also helps you feel confident, focused, committed, decisive and full of belief before you hit the ball and after it leaves the clubface.

Finally in this section we will discuss the art and science of a winning mentality. The targets you set yourself for competition golf and the mindset you experience as you actually compete collide and interact. The goals you have leading into a tournament shape your temperament and your ability to focus. They affect your emotional control and capability to maintain high confidence. We close section two by establishing a competition mindset – one that affords you the very best opportunity to shoot low no matter what the arena you confront.

Perform

And the arena is where it counts.

In golf your arena is vast – usually well over 100 acres in size. And the golf stadium is dynamic and changing. It's full of natural hazards and man-made obstacles. It is subject to the elements of sun and wind and rain. It's unpredictable in its bounce and erratic in its kicks. And you have to perform in it.

To do this you have to take control. You have to take control of you. You have to learn how to handle yourself, your mindset, and your physiology for over three hours, across 18 holes, no matter what the conditions, no matter what the opposition, no matter what the type of competition.

Self-management could be *the* hidden mediator of performance - the silent determinant of success. A mind on the ball and a mind on self

Introduction

meets the two primary challenges of golf – get the ball in the hole in as few strokes as possible by being the best *you* that *you* can be every second, every minute and every hour you compete. Section three teaches you how to be the 'best you' as you stride the course. It teaches you to take control.

Endlessly frustrating, never perfectible, your brain and nervous system do battle to capture your attention. They send signals to distract and to judge. They launch a verbal volley of abuse through your thinking. They accelerate your heart rate when holes look tough. They shoot emotion through your body that breaks out into feelings hindering your swing and your touch. To be Golf Tough means taking control of these factors; factors that impede your scoring potential. It means taking charge of the mental elements that settle your brain and nervous system, encouraging great shots and sprinkles of birdies.

You, feeling good on the course - feeling great even - will be our driving creed.

To do this you need a self-management blueprint that helps you steer mind and body effectively. Having a catalogue of techniques to draw upon, under pressure, is a must-have in any champion's armoury.

We will explore your personal controllers – your body language and your self-talk. Having a structure to your thinking and to your actions during the downtime, as you walk from your first shot to your second, and as you stroll from fairway to green, is essential. It is during the quiet moments that the brain so often makes its noise - so much time to think, to dwell and to ruminate. Perhaps the true essence of competitive golf is the ability to perform in the time in-between the action. The golfer needs to manage his inner demons as he paces the fairway.

And with a mental structure, that method of thinking and doing and being (neatly tucked under your arm), all that is left to do is to keep doing the right things time and time again. Repetition and reinforcement are the guardians of excellence. Champion golfers obsess over learning, development and improvement. They are relentless purveyors of progression.

Progress

To me the art of mental toughness is playing through the uncomfortable. Perhaps this is also the art of progression in golf - to drive forward when the tank is empty, to energise yourself when all seems lost, to maintain enthusiasm no matter what.

Golf is a game of inconsistency. One day you feel you've got it nailed, the next, it's on the wane. It's also a game of plateau. That upward curve of improvement never lasts for long, it soon flattens and you find yourself having to unearth new ways to evolve. To develop, to improve, to learn, to establish effective habits and patterns – these are the attitudinal cornerstones of champion golfers. And these qualities must remain in place irrespective of the state of your golf, irrespective of the score you've just shot, and irrespective of the speed of your trajectory.

Progression is, to some extent, a state of mind. We can *all* improve. There may be some people who are born with a pre-disposition to play great golf. There may be others who will always find the feeling of standing over the golf ball uncomfortable and alien. But we can *all* get better. We can't all be scratch golfers but we can all strive to touch par as often as possible. And despite some God given restrictions, and despite some time limitations, I believe that if you make the decision to find out how good you can really be, you'll surprise yourself. Everyone has a golfing brain that has the capacity to develop and grow.

This fourth section of Golf Tough provides you with a template for progression. It starts with a microscopic look at the game within the game – putting. It's a devilishly difficult compartment of golf, one that tests nerves, and one where the slightest tension punishes severely. Arguably it is on the putting green where you need to be at your strongest mentally. It's when the immediacy of success and failure is most potent – you hole it or you miss it, there is no other outcome, there are no ifs, buts, or maybes. Despite its complexity putting is a fundamental of Golf Tough and I strongly believe every golfer needs a keen sense of how to improve their putting and how to execute their stroke under pressure. It requires a delicate interaction between mentality and technique - one that we will address here.

Introduction

In chapter 12 I will introduce you to a number of practical techniques to develop your psychological skills on and off the course. Perhaps my toughest job as a golf psychologist is helping players, particularly highly driven ones, find their motivational sweetspot. The optimal mindset is one that balances focus and freedom, intensity and relaxation, and effort and patience. Somewhere in the middle sits the window to progression.

Chapter 13 reflects this mixed complex landscape – no one ever said performance psychology was straightforward. Your ability to progress your golf isn't just mediated by 'being positive'. Sure, being positive and optimistic is an overarching trait of a champion, but, on occasion, being ready to compete and being able to progress require the complete opposite. It's useful to embrace a time of negative thinking. Asking yourself, "If it goes wrong, what will I do?" is a question that will help you strategise and ready you for the adversity that golf inevitably delivers. A balance of optimism and pessimism primes your golfing mind and body to play Golf Tough.

How to Read This Book

There is no real beginning to this book. The theme of 'Practice' enjoys pride of place in the first section of Golf Tough because working on your game diligently and correctly is so often overlooked and can impact your scores emphatically. But feel free to dive into any section. I'd like to think that every chapter offers a few nuggets to take into your next competitive outing.

Golf Tough is littered with the tales and tools of golf coaches and playing professionals who continue to support my own growth as a sport psychologist. Spending just half an hour with them can have more impact on your golf game than a week of practice at the range. They have been kind enough to share their insights and have allowed me to sprinkle Golf Tough with the kind of stories that bring the sporting mindset and the golf brain alive.

Be proactive as you read. Exercise your thinking. Look up from this book regularly and access your memory stores. Are your thoughts, feelings and behaviours on the course, and on the practice ground, those of a champion? Assign some downtime to analyse your performance thinking – really get to know you, the golfer. Then stretch yourself. Come out of your comfort zone. Work hard to adopt some of the approaches that are suggested in this book.

Everything written in Golf Tough is simple. But there is a difference between simple and easy. Acclimatising to the mannerisms of a champion won't be easy. Golf is hard and sometimes cruel. Any game that is subject to the whims of the weather, the layout of the land, the play of the opposition and the quirks of the brain is likely to prove elusive. As a player then coach and now psychologist I've seen clubs thrown, clubs broken, and clubs binned.

Golf, the game we love, does this to people. It is frustrating and infuriating but equally uplifting, energising and addictive. It offers a melting pot of mixed emotion. It can scramble the hardiest of minds. But you can learn to manage your mindset. You can indeed learn to be the best *you* that *you* can be, if not all of the time, then at least most of the time. No matter what your age and no matter what your level, you can learn to be Golf Tough. You can learn to play Golf Tough.

 Please note: included in the text are some of the Tweets I post on Twitter that aim to get golfers discussing performance and mindset. I hope you find them thought-provoking.

1

A Numbers Game

He sees the game differently.

He has a brain that churns numbers and a brain that deals in probability. He can reduce golf to a set of figures but he can also find meaning behind the data.

There is the ball, there is the hole – but to him every shot played has significance aside from simple birdies, pars and bogeys. Every shot has a consequence that impacts not only your score, but also your approach to the game, to your practice habits and your mindset.

He treads the turf of global golf as a silent persuader. He knows the game like you don't. In fact, he knows the subtle nuances of golf better than the gladiators themselves. He has captivated some of the world's best players by showing them the real impact their numbers have on their results. He has enthralled some of the game's leading teachers with his knowledge and understanding of the quiet predictors of success.

When he speaks people listen. Good players and great players pay attention. They focus because they know a golden nugget can help them shoot a better score or win a bigger cheque. In a game of centimetres he's the invaluable source of information that can make the difference – that can help to make the cut, finish top three, or birdie the last to keep a Tour card.

This is the story of the world's leading golf statistician. And there is plenty you can learn from him that will take your game in the right direction.

The Story of Sellsie

Chris Sells had a dream. He wanted to be a professional golfer. In fact, he wanted to be the best golfer in the world.

A studious teenager with a gift for mathematics, he used his love of numbers to his advantage. Whilst his mates measured their rounds through birdies and bogeys Chris (or Sellsie to friends) looked beyond the scorecard for answers to improve his golf. He started to examine the evidence that determined the numbers on his scorecard – essentially the numbers that delivered the numbers.

Over a couple of years he committed himself to developing a library of statistics on his game. He kept a record of the number of fairways and greens he hit as well as how many putts he made. Nothing revolutionary, but these simple stats helped him learn more about the key performance indicators that he needed to work on. His commitment to this process helped him win his Club Championship – a competition that had a strong selection of scratch and plus-handicap golfers.

Sellsie would cite a lack of hand-eye coordination as his main obstacle to playing professional golf – he came to realise he'd never quite be good enough to compete on the pro circuit. So, after college, he entered the family business and played the game competitively, but primarily for fun. Working in a family environment he found he had quite a bit of breathing space to play golf, but instead of playing he chose to head out on the European Amateur circuit and watch his two best mates, John Franks and Mark Side, compete. As he watched, he kept stats, and both players became curious about the information Sellsie carried with him from tournament to tournament. Both asked him to sit with them and explain the significance of their statistics to them. This request gave Sellsie an idea.

Keen to know more about the impact the underlying numbers have on a golfer's score, Sellsie immersed himself in researching the games of the best golfers to ever hold a club. He became passionate about detecting the ingredients for golf champions, right up to a prolific Major winner. He asked the questions that fascinated him, then number-crunched the answers.

- How many putts does a professional miss inside 6 feet?
- What percentage of putts should you hole from outside 25 feet?
- Is accuracy more important than distance?
- Do you have any club defects in your bag?
- Are three wedges better than four?
- Will doing lots of bunker practice actually help your scoring?

He also extended his research towards amateur golfers. More questions emerged.

- What are the key differences between scratch golfers and five handicappers?
- On average how many greens does a ten handicapper have to hit to break 80?
- Is it possible for a fifteen handicapper to putt as well as a professional?
- What should a twenty handicapper specifically work on to get his / her handicap down?

Sellsie laboured over the next few years to build an enviable understanding of the link between statistics, performance, and outcomes. His blend of knowledge about the amateur and professional game soon caught the interest of the English Golf Union and he was quickly rewarded with a contract to work as their performance analyst. His eye for detail impressed the most sceptical of golfers and it wasn't long until the best players in the game became curious. Sellsie started working with European Tour professionals David Howell and Paul McGinley, providing them with week-to-week information on the state of their games. He has subsequently gone on to work with numerous golf organisations (including equipment manufacturers and the PGA European Tour) as well as dozens of leading coaches and over 50 of the world's best players.

Alongside his work on the global Professional Tours, Sellsie's passion has been to help the everyday golfer. So he set up an online platform called *strokeaverage.com* to help players, no matter what their level, record their statistics and plot their way to lower scores. And it is the combination of his efforts with the game's elite, and the figures he has derived from competitors at the grassroots of golf, that has enabled

Sellsie to find patterns in the data that should not and cannot be ignored.

Here is what Sellsie knows. This is what I believe.

Golf Rule Number One

Sellsie and I have a new 'Golf Rule Number One' for you. It has nothing to do with grip or stance or swing plane. It doesn't involve lie or conditions or temperament. It is rarely written about in the pages of an instruction book, yet its detail informs your golfing journey and enlightens you on the necessities to reach your destination.

Quite simply you *must* keep your golfing stats. If you want to be a scratch golfer you *must* keep stats. If you want to reduce your handicap to single figures you *must* keep stats. If you want to play with the world's best golfers it is *imperative* that you keep your stats.

How many golfers keep their statistics? I'm unsure - probably less than 0.1%. Yet how many golfers moan and groan about their latest competitive round? How many golfers are willing to go spend hundreds of dollars on the latest driver? How many golfers are willing to take time to go beat balls at the range in the hope of improvement? I would say more than 0.1%.

To my mind keeping statistics is a progression and performance fundamental that golfers too often ignore. Storing your numbers will speed your improvement and support a more consistent game. Let me give you a few reasons why.

Effective practice starts by keeping your statistics. Numbers tell you the truth about your game.

Stats Drive Practice and Preparation

Without stats you are blind to the improvements you need to make. I see this blindness on the driving range. Golfers hitting bucket after bucket without really knowing whether the long game is the area they need to improve, to lower their scores, or not. Most golfers practice the game akin to playing darts blindfolded. Your ability to throw the dart isn't impeded, but who knows what part of the board you'll hit. By all means take time to practice your golf game, but do so with knowledge of the specific areas you *need* to improve. You'll limit your ability to lower your scores if you don't. You'll limit your ability to play Golf Tough if you ignore the numbers.

Keeping detailed statistics of the rounds you play is your entry point to precision practice. The data helps fix your mind on the area of your game that is most in need of improvement. Stats form patterns over time, so rather than holding a vague belief about the state of a specific part of your game you'll be able to *pinpoint* components that are letting you down. You'll develop a firm grasp of the minutiae underpinning your competitive scores. Holding concrete data is important because the brain needs some guidance; its quirks, otherwise, will send you in the wrong direction.

Quirks of the Brain

If you decide against keeping statistics, yet you still want to improve and play Golf Tough, you'll have a problem. Your brain, that most powerful of machines, functions according to two peculiarities that will dictate what you remember about your rounds and subsequently emphasise what you supposedly 'know' about your game.

If I was to rattle off a string of, say, 15 digits and ask you to recall them, scientific research has shown that you'll find it easiest to recollect the final few digits. You'll likely remember and reflect back to me those last couple of digits first. This sounds obvious doesn't it, yet this phenomenon, called the *recency effect*, influences many aspects of our lives. It impacts our behaviours and attitudes, how we feel about someone as well as the things we choose to believe in. It is a strategy marketers use to help us make our purchasing choices.

The recency effect can bias the opinions you hold about your golf game. Finish the round with a few missed putts or some wild tee shots and you'll likely regale 19th hole regulars about your putting woes or your driving inaccuracies. As we shall come to discuss, the story you tell yourself about your golf influences how you see your game and how you feel about it. The recency effect can skew your innermost beliefs about your performances.

Emotion also plays a part in determining your thoughts about your game. As a general rule, we remember emotionally charged events better than boring ones. And the memory of strongly emotional moments may shove and shift the memory of less emotional information out of conscious awareness. So you may be less likely to remember information if it is followed by something that delivers a powerful emotional response.

What does this mean for the golfer? Any putt, chip, approach shot, or drive which is followed by a rush of emotion lingers in the mind. It can distort any judgement of performance after the round. Emotion can put a twist on a round that leaves a golfer finding fault in the wrong direction.

As a consultant I find both these idiosyncrasies of the brain a frequent problem. A client blames his putting because he 'felt' like he hit a lot of putts and left a lot of putts hanging on the lip. With obedience to this feeling the client decides to spend the following week hitting a lot of putts. He ignores other areas of his game because he believes it necessary to go fix things on the practice putting green. Yet, when we get around to writing out and examining his stats, we notice a different story. We notice that, whilst he hit a fair number of fairways and greens in regulation, he only had one first putt from within 10 feet. Most approach shots had finished 20 to 50 feet from the hole. No wonder he felt like he hit a lot of putts – he had left himself a whole pile of work to do to two putt his greens in regulation! And further analysis showed that when he missed the green most of the time his chips finished more than six feet away from the hole. He had put enormous pressure on his short putting. He had gotten especially frustrated with the two missed putts from 6 and 12 feet on the final two holes.

So what has this common example exposed about my client? That he had incorrectly identified putting as his primary weakness when, in fact, it was his approach play that needed work. He needed to hit a greater number of shots closer to the flag to give himself a better chance of holing the subsequent putts and shoot a lower score. His chipping could do with some practice as well. The impact that the recency effect (as well as biased emotion) can have on memory had taken hold. A failure to keep stats meant that he acted on the 'feeling' he derived from his performance and his subsequent decision to spend the next week working on his putting was incorrect. Falling into this trap once in a while may be fine, but if he wants to learn to play Golf Tough he needs to be consistent in keeping his game statistics and act according to the data rather than practice on a whim.

Be careful what you remember about your round – memory isn't always truth!

No Stats, Less Informed Coaching

Statistics not only inform the golfer about the specific areas he needs to focus on and practice, they also support the coaching process.

Some years ago I used to make a living from teaching golf. Players competing at all levels would come for a lesson. They did so because they wanted to improve – to break 90 or 80, or maybe even 70. The goal was usually clear. But more often than not the process of improvement was ambiguous. Where exactly are you now with your game, and what specifically do we need to improve to reach your end in mind?

Historically, club professionals and teaching assistants have escorted pupils out to the range to beat balls. Fault fixing the swing has always been the traditional entry point to improving someone's game. But how effective is this route? Who is to say that a swing change will shoot a 69, 79, or 89? In my own coaching practice I'd do my best to take a pupil through a battery of questions - I needed to know the ins and outs of their game in order to help them lower their scores. But there is a better way to learn the strengths and weaknesses of someone's golf.

Keeping statistics on a system like strokeaverage.com helps you and your professional coach co-create a set of solutions that help you build the game of your dreams. Together you can identify the patterns that hold you back. If your coach sees that you're holing just 20% of putts from 7 feet to 12 feet then he will know that one of his remits will be to take you to the putting green. If he spots that you have a tendency to miss the green on the left his instruction can be tailored towards such a problem (possibly even recommending an equipment check for defects).

There is, of course, the argument that the higher your handicap the more generic your challenges are. But there are still game differences between high handicappers. Some players fail to break 90 because of a poor short game, whilst others struggle to get it off the tee. Handing over your statistics to your coach means that his teaching improves – he can be more precise and his assessment is less about guesswork. Intuition will always be a part of his coaching armoury, but raw data aids training insight. Help *him* help *you*!

No Stats, Less Confidence

Let's use our imagination.

About six months ago you decided, with your coach, that you needed to improve your mid-range putting and your pitching from 20 to 80 yards out. You were only holing 20% of putts from 7 to 12 feet and your pitches were finishing an average of 25 feet from the flag from this short range distance.

So you got to work with your coach on the technical aspects of your putting stroke, developed a more consistent putting routine and started to practice your stroke both at your home club and indoors in your office. You also started to dedicate a little more time to your pitching. Realising you never really practiced this area of the game, you agreed with your coach that, rather than reach for the driver on your weekly visit to the range, you would spend more time hitting some wedges. You decided to hit 10 wedges to a 20 yard target, 10 wedges to a 40 yard target, 10 to 60, and 10 to 80 yards.

You committed to this practice plan for a couple of months. You still played competitively and kept your statistics and last month you took the opportunity to check out your latest data. The numbers had changed. You had improved to 30% of putts holed from 7 to 12 feet, and your average distance from the flag when pitching from 20 to 80 yards was closer at 19 feet.

This is a beautiful shift – the most perfect form of confidence building. It's based on evidence. It's based on tangible data that you can *see*. A hit of adrenaline and a boost of confidence are inevitable when you *know* your game has improved. There's no guesswork, there's no conjecture. You can *see* it in black and white.

Statistics help you to *know* about your game. When your stats move in a positive direction they help you to *know* something has improved. You can't get a better confidence building system than that.

The highest form of confidence is to 'know'. I am confident I can, I believe I can, I KNOW I can...

Statistics – the What, the How, and the Interpretation

When one of Sellsie's clients tees it up at a big tournament, whether it's Graeme McDowell, Anders Hansen or Rory McIlroy, it is likely that their caddies will be keeping their numbers. It is the player's responsibility to note down the scores, but the caddy may record the data related to specific shots.

Of course the vast majority of golfers reading this book won't have the luxury of having a bag carrier to note down the numbers. It's something you will probably have to do yourself. But this is a fairly easy process to commit to.

What and How

There are numerous ways to record your stats, with the easiest and most effective being to enter the data as you play. To do this, take a notebook onto the course with you. Make sure it's small enough to fit into your back pocket. For each shot, keep a record of:

- The type of shot hit; e.g. tee / advancing shot / approach / chip / putt
- The club used; e.g. Driver / 3 wood / 6 iron / Pitching Wedge

- The direction the ball finishes in relation to the target; e.g. left / right / short / through the green
- The end lie; e.g. on the green / on the fairway / in the semi-rough / in the trees
- The estimated length of putts; e.g. 1 foot / 15 feet / 40 feet

To avoid disrupting play, try to note down your data whilst others are hitting or while walking to your next shot. You can, of course, record stats after the round has finished, or even commit to a combination of recording some shots on the course and some after you've played – choose a system that is most comfortable for you.

It's particularly important that the data you extract from putting is accurate as it's so easy to skew the statistics from careless measurements. Pay precise attention to the length of your shorter putts of 15 feet and under – it's easy to be out by a foot or two. To gauge the distances of longer putts Tour caddies often take the time to pace the length. This can be done quickly and without disruption provided you don't stand on anyone's line.

A helpful tip to improve your ability to judge putt lengths is to practice becoming acquainted with your exact stride length on the practice putting green. The simple use of a piece of string will suffice. Measure out 3, 6, 10, 15 and 20 feet, then walk next to the string and get a feel for how long your normal walking pace is. An average step would be about 3 feet per pace, but everyone is a little different according to size and walking style.

To measure the distance of your approach shots I recommend using course guides or the markers to the side of the fairways. However, with technology influencing today's modern game more and more, golfers are using yardage binoculars or satellite navigation systems. Buying a visual aid or downloading an app can offer an effective way of ensuring you are recording accurate distances.

Like many things in life, success can be found by committing to detail. Commit to keeping your numbers on the course. Whilst your main focus should be on your golf and playing to the very best of your ability, do allow some head space to record your data. Once you've collected it there are plenty of systems out there such as Sellsie's strokeaverage.com that can help you store your stats. After you've kept a few rounds you can collate the information you hold and start to interpret the data.

The Interpretation

Congratulations! Your journey towards golfing excellence, perhaps even Golf Tough is underway. You are keeping your statistics and you now have a record of the shots you are hitting on the course. But keeping them is one thing, acting on them is another - you now need to start upskilling your golf by pinpointing areas that need improving.

There are two roads to take once you have a keen understanding of your golf statistics. Your first is to identify your two worst data points and set about improving these specific areas. The second option is to isolate a single long game and short game area to cover both bases. The path you choose depends on your standard and the specific numbers that confront you. In general, players with less ability should choose long and short game components, while better golfers ought to opt for their two inferior statistics.

This period of data examination is the time you ask the question 'why' and then spend a short period searching for answers. Allow me to use an example from putting. You notice that you are leaving long putts quite a distance from the hole. Putts struck from over 20 feet are being left further than 3 feet from the hole a mammoth 50% of the time. Here come the questions: Is your challenge a technical one? Perhaps you're not getting a consistent enough strike on the ball? Or maybe your putting tempo is a little inconsistent leaving putts short and long? Are you reading the green incorrectly? Could it be that you need a lesson on green reading to sharpen your eyes for the sloped contoured surface? Could it be more of a mental problem? Perhaps you rush these pace putts? Maybe you need to establish a way to foster an improved focus? Or perhaps you just need to practice a little more and build some confidence with the flat stick from distance?

Ideally, use a qualified PGA golf professional to interpret your data. They will ask the right questions – the kind that opens up a catalogue of internal pictures in your mind's eye. They bring the numbers to life. 55% of putts holed from inside 6 feet isn't just a figure to be looked at

– it fronts a set of thoughts and a bunch of behaviours that can help you improve. Just as night follows day, so your poorest statistical numbers will follow a specific error in your game. A PGA coach will help you unpick the good from the bad.

If you do employ a coach to help your game then this is something they will probably insist on doing anyway. Accept his or her help – connecting with someone who is knowledgeable about *your* game and *the* game will help you sort through your statistics quickly and effectively.

It's easy to go on. I could fill a book on the performance components that underpin and mediate the numbers. The point is - you need the numbers in the first place to start improving your golf. You need the numbers to learn, to develop and improve. And you need the numbers to explore just how good you can be and whether you can play Golf Tough.

Improvement in golf doesn't happen by accident. Improvement is a process. And it starts with game knowledge.

The Point Is...

Your path to excellence, no matter what your personal ambition looks like, begins with a set of numbers. When you can sit in the quiet of your home and allow a wave of belief to flow through you (because you can see a positive shift in the data that underpin your game) then you can build Golf Tough. Make these numbers big and bold and bright. Blow them up in your mind. They are important. They are your feel good digits that allow you to express your confidence on the golf course.

If your numbers aren't the best, that's fine. See this as the start of a new exciting chapter in your golfing journey. You are going to set about improving your data set. You now know *where* you need to extend your effort - it's time to act on this knowledge.

Statistics are a true depiction of your ability. They calmly reflect back the facts. But they are so much more than truth. They can be used as your confidence rocket fuel. Improve your numbers and you'll release a hit of adrenaline into your nervous system. A positive movement is a cause for celebration. A positive nudge in numbers is worth ten times the wise words of a sport psychologist. By committing to building superior figures you give yourself the evidence and the ammunition to grace the tee *knowing* that you *can*.

If you want to play Golf Tough, it is important, from time to time, to turn up the volume of emotion on this quiet game of ours. Bring your numbers alive. Create a fist pump from your series of stats. I know Sellsie would approve. And I know he'd like you to do something with those numbers. He'd like them to shape your practice plan. Let's explore how you can do this.

2

Becoming Skilful

The life of a professional touring golf coach isn't just nomadic, it can be frustrating too. Great coaching doesn't automatically mean that clients will register a win or pick up a good cheque - results are out of the coach's control. Saying the right thing, at the right time, isn't a guarantee of success and the correct diagnoses of any swing faults are not a shoe-in for an under par round. Coaches need to be Golf Tough too!

The Tour coach leads an inconsistent life travelling between countries, rarely seeing sights outside the hotel and golf course. This lifestyle is seldom rewarded with riches - that's the player's reserve. But coaches don't necessarily do it for the cash. Most do it for that addictive feeling of helping. They do it for the buzz of emotion when their player goes on a birdie streak or plays unstoppable golf. They do it because seeing that little white ball disappear into the hole as a result of some of their input is, for them, a very sweet feeling.

For Tour coach Hugh Marr, travelling from tournament to tournament isn't so bad. He has some important time fillers. This period 'in-between' events is when he does much of his game analysis – it's a stage for productivity. It is when he has downtime at the airport, or on the plane, that he can really get to grips with his client's game. With a laptop in front of him he can assess and interpret a player's data. He can find the clues that may unlock a good week for one of his competitors.

As a modern coach Hugh isn't obsessed with, or blinded by, technique. Sure, he understands the swing as well as any global golf coach, but he appreciates that technique is only a part of the equation of golfing excellence and not the only platform where champions spring from. He is, first and foremost, preoccupied by a player's golf data - the interpretation of statistics and the most effective way of delivering improvement based on the numbers. It is his treatment of data that forms the bedrock of his relationship with clients. He is then focused on helping them develop the skill they need to play the golf of their dreams. Crunch the stats, find the weaknesses, and start to build the skill that will upgrade their game. This is Hugh Marr's system. This is his philosophy. It is compelling, it is enduring, it is based on sound coaching science and it can help you.

The Travelling Scotsman

Golf statistics may well be the only thing that is consistent in the professional life of Hugh Marr. One week he is heading up Surrey Golf Lab, a technologically driven golf studio in Surrey, England, whereas the next week he is jetting out to a European or global destination to help the games of one of his Tour clients. During other weeks he is on lead coach duties for the very successful England Under-18 golf team at sleepy Woodhall Spa Golf Club, in the heart of the country. Hugh is a busy man, and he clocks up plenty of air miles!

His scientific, evidence-based, approach is in stark contrast to his upbringing. As a youth in Glasgow he shunned school, leaving at 17 to pursue a career in golf. With a 9 handicap and one of his teachers declaring that he had more chance of being an astronaut than a pro golfer he wasn't deterred – within a year he had a scratch handicap!

Over the next decade Hugh built a strong reputation as a golf coach. Based at the exclusive Wisley Golf Club just outside London he became Surrey County head coach (helping them win three national titles) and, with plenty of success at local level, he started to draw interest from several European Tour players. Things have flown from there.

Hugh's love for learning never abates. He reads widely on topics such as physics, psychology, biomechanics, and physical fitness – all of which informs how he goes about helping his clients. His knowledge of anatomy related to golf swing mechanics is first class, and it is this acquaintance with the body relative to the swing that sets him apart from his peers.

However, it is his interest in skill acquisition and his approach to developing skill that we will home in on in this chapter. Above all else, Hugh and I want you to build skill, and we know how to help you do so. To explain further, let's take a lesson with Hugh Marr.

A Lesson with Hugh

He didn't say much for 45 minutes. But I could see him looking. I could feel his eyes scanning motion and outcome. We were at Reigate Hill Golf Club, home to Hugh's Surrey Golf Lab, and I'd been set a challenge. I was playing one of Hugh's skills tests. I was focused and having fun. Above all I was learning!

The '9 Shot Challenge' game is one of the toughest of the dozens of skills tests Hugh monitors whenever his pupils visit him at the lab. He wants to see how they perform under pressure. He wants to see their reaction to failure, to success, and he wants to help them learn under stress. His skills tests are his stress tests.

My challenge was simple – hit 9 shots with a 6 iron, and 9 with a driver. But each shot had to vary slightly – a straight shot played high, normal, and knockdown. A draw shot played into a specific target area high, normal, and low running. Finally, a fade shot played high, then normal, and one with a low launch. After I had struck all 9 we added up my score and I was then asked to execute the same demanding flights and trajectories with a driver.

As I progressed with the test Hugh asked me to go through my routine. He said little, standing behind and to the side, observing my behaviour moving into the ball, noticing the way my club worked back and through, and listening to the sound the ball made off the clubface. I, myself, saw Hugh briefly checking the ball's flight and outcome, ticking or crossing his clipboard as I progressed through the test.

Once through the 18 different shots, Hugh asked me to repeat the test – he is renowned for really pushing the players he works with.

Like many good modern day coaches, when you arrive for a lesson Hugh doesn't automatically ask you to reach for your 7 iron. He doesn't assume you want a long game session and he doesn't presume that your technique needs fixing.

Go for a lesson with Hugh and you may start by looking at your statistics together. If you don't have any (most don't) then Hugh will talk to you a little about your game – he'll ask you the right questions and you'll uncover the areas you need to work on in order to improve your game. At this stage, depending on the specific challenge you have, it's unlikely he'll dive straight into working on your swing or stroke mechanics. Instead he'll probably set up a skills test for you to accomplish. He wants to see you in action under pressure. This is because Hugh knows there is a difference between technique and skill. Most people don't!

Golf Skill versus Golf Technique

Technique is the ability to perform a physical task, whereas skill is the ability to perform a task in a game setting. This is a subtle yet cavernous difference that seems to have bypassed many golfers – from recreational, through to good amateurs, as well as professionals. It is one that shouldn't be ignored.

Developing golf technique is different to developing golf skill. Technique is a component of skill - that is all. Technique doesn't win trophies, nor does it reduce your handicap by five shots. Technique doesn't hole putts and it doesn't help players graduate to Tour standard. Technique is only a *part* of the process.

Golf demands the ability to control the ball over an ever-changing terrain in an ever-changing environment. And competitive golf demands you do this, under pressure. Isolating the golf swing and working on it is not the golf course formula for success. It's the practice ground formula for success. Training yourself to hit from one spot with one motion is not golf skill. It's driving range skill. Training yourself to stroke from one spot with one motion is not putting skill. It's practice putting green skill.

Too many golfers incorrectly believe that within lower handicaps lies better technique. And too many golfers believe that the only way to shoot lower scores is to improve their technique. Wrong and wrong!

Let me be very clear. I am *not* saying that technique is irrelevant. I am *not* suggesting that technical excellence isn't the mainstay of champion golfers. Having a repeatable motion is important, and this is why the next chapter is dedicated to the psychology of developing your swing and stroke technique. I am *not* anti-technique. Refuting its importance would be like denying the presence of the sun and moon and sky.

What I *am* arguing is that to be the very best golfer you can be, you need to practice in a manner that helps you improve your golf skill and not just your swing and stroke technique. You need to be able to package your technique so that you can transfer it onto the first tee under competition pressure. You need to practice in a manner that focuses your mind and builds confidence. These are essential acquisitions as you work towards being Golf Tough.

The most effective form of practice is one that puts *you* at the heart of the learning process. It demands more from you than to simply hit a position in the swing. It is not necessarily the attainment of one motion or one action. It is called skills testing, and here is its art and science.

Practice with the focus of play, and you'll play with the freedom of practice.

Skills Testing – The Art from the Science

I'm going to give you two scenarios. I want you to pick which you think is the most effective platform for improving your golf.

In scenario 1, I want you to put yourself on your local driving range. You've chosen a big bucket of balls – 100 of them. You've got an hour or so to get through them - plenty of time to hit lots of shots. And that is what you do, you hit shot after shot. When you hit them straight you get a rush of adrenaline and you quickly scoop up another ball to repeat the swing that's led to a mini success. When you hit shots left and right, or duff or thin, you berate yourself and strive to focus better on the next one. Despite the inconsistency you're putting effort in. You're practicing hard. That is how games are won right? By practicing hard!

In scenario 2, I want you to once again put yourself on your local driving range. This time you've chosen a small bucket of balls – 60 of them. Like our first scene you have about an hour to hit them, but this time you're going to create a skills test – an assessment that will tax your mind and body. You're going to put yourself under a little bit of pressure because you know that's what the *game* demands. The test you decide to do is called the 'Tee Shot Challenge' (it's one of Hugh's). You want to test your tee shots because they've been a little off lately. You mark out a fairway twenty yards wide by using the flags that are on the range and you give yourself an extra 5 yards either side of the flags to denote the semi rough. The game is simple – using your driver, 3 wood, and a hybrid or long iron, you hit thirty shots in total (ten each) and give yourself 3 points for a fairway hit, 2 points if the ball finishes in the semi rough, and minus 1 point for a missed fairway. Once you've completed this you do it again and strive to beat your first attempt.

Let's briefly discuss the difference between the two scenes. Their distinction is striking! The approach in scene 1 lacks structure and bears little relation to playing golf on the course. More often than not it will fail to capture the interest of the golfer for the duration of the practice time and acts as a catalyst for a rollercoaster ride of emotion. The golfer can build confidence from a session like this if he hits it well, but down to chance more so than design. Most importantly scene 1 puts no pressure on the golfer – there is no emphasis or measurement of success and failure.

In contrast, scene 2 details a game that is fun to complete (and fun is a forerunner to focus). The 'Tee Shot Challenge' is a skills test that puts you under pressure – it mirrors the actual skill you have to execute on the course. Sure, you may experience negative emotion if you perform badly, but this gives you the opportunity to learn to keep your cool. If you succeed in beating your previous attempts on the test you'll receive a huge hit of confidence as you walk away from the range. You will have *seen* progress. You will have *proof* that you are developing skill. If, on the other hand, your score deteriorates on a third, fourth or fifth attempt, that's fine as well. If there is a pattern to your misses then seek out your PGA coach for some help. He may be able to give you some technical pointers that will enhance your skill building. Combining your coach's technical instruction with your skills tests – now there's a compelling double act.

Do skills tests help you learn? Do they help you improve? Of course they do. They help you develop the hand-eye coordination you need to play Golf Tough. They help you learn to play under pressure. They target specific improvement related to the on-course areas you are testing.

Skill isn't just technique. It's a heady mix of confidence and focus. It's coordination. It's attuning mind with body. It's training your brain to react to a target without thought or over-complication. It's feeling the swing and linking the kinaesthetic to seeing the outcome. It puts you in the pilot seat. It avoids an over-reliance on your coach or your playing partner or a parent or spouse. After all, they won't be able to do it for you on the course in a competitive environment. Skilled golf under pressure is down to you and you alone. That, as a student of Golf Tough, is your privilege *and* your burden.

Ultimately, the golfer who takes home the trophy is the one who executed the most skill under pressure.

Your Skills Tests

A skills test is nothing more than a game – a game to test and challenge and tease. It's a game that's fun, but it's not frivolous – it can focus your mind and frustrate in equal measure.

A test narrows the game down to a specific component such as putting or tee shots, although you can create skills tests that mix different areas of golf. A test that comprises both chipping and putting, or which fuses driving and approach shots, can create more realism and a greater challenge.

The essence of skills tests is to 'train the whole'. They are designed to train your thinking, your feelings and your actions. This combination is imperative because the three collide on the golf course as you compete. Your thoughts influence your actions and both thought and action mediate how you feel. A circular momentum is established between these three human qualities that vibrate back and forth. To play Golf Tough you have to strive to manage all three.

Here are some example tests to help you build skill, to put you under pressure and to help you build confidence. Some are the tests Hugh uses with his Tour professional clients, whilst some are mine.

Putting – 'Par 5' (A Hugh Marr Skill Test)

Isolate a hole on the putting green and measure 18 inches to the sides of the cup (left and right) and 18 inches behind it. Mark out this area using a couple of tees.

Now measure out 5 specific distances from the hole – 6 feet, 12 feet, 18 feet, 24 feet and 30 feet. Place a ball at each location.

You are going to putt from each spot keeping a score using this system – hole the ball to go one under par; leave the ball short to make a double bogey (2 over); if the ball finishes level with the hole or inside the marked zone you make par (your par zone); race the ball past the hole and the par zone and you drop a shot (1 over).

Add up your score – it would be great if you finish under par. After you've completed your first go, immediately set about trying to beat your initial score. If you get to the final few putts and you have to putt the ball into the marked zone you'll find yourself getting a little edgy. You may experience nerves as such, but you may get a little tight in your body and a little tentative with your stroke. It's a perfect putting skills test to recreate the sensations you have as you compete on the course.

Pitching – 'All the 10's'

Mark out an area 10 feet in radius around a flag (or, if you are a less proficient player, 15-20 feet).

Place 10 balls 20 yards from the flag, 10 balls 30 yards away, and 10 balls 40 yards from the flag. Never hit consecutive shots from one distance – move up and down the line so you get to experience a different distance with each shot you make.

The aim of this test is to hit the 10 foot green as often as you can. You can set yourself a target of between 20 to 25 hits (about 70% to 80%).

To put more pressure on yourself, narrow the target, or raise the goal, and keep re-testing.

The more hits you experience as you narrow your target the more confident you will feel with your pitching. If, however, you consistently fail then it might be time to take a pitching lesson. Do this test with your PGA professional next to you. Watching you will help him find appropriate technical solutions for your pitching set up and action.

Driving – 'Off the Tee'

This test is great at building frustration (and thus helpful not just as a skills builder but also as a test for managing emotions). It takes discipline, determination, and dedication to complete it.

Take 10 balls and pick out a fairway 20 yards wide. Use different objects such as marker boards, flags, or even trees on the range to do this.

The aim of this test is simple - hit as many consecutive shots onto the fairway as possible. If you miss a fairway then you have to start your count again.

This test is pressure laden. Your objective is to hit all 10 shots onto a fairway – the seventh, eighth, ninth and tenth balls will be heavily burdened by stress. Negative thoughts will probably pop into your mind as you reach the latter stages – "Don't miss now, I've nearly completed the test." A great way to learn how to manage your brain and nervous system while experiencing competitive anxiety.

Long Game - 'Fairways and Greens' (A Hugh Marr Skills Test)

This is a great test to acquaint yourself with keeping statistics.

Play 9 holes on the range but limit them to tee shots and approaches. Give yourself a point for hitting the fairway and a point for hitting the green. Also, reward yourself with additional points for hitting your intended shots, for example a draw, fade, or straight shot.

This skills test is a great way to prepare for an upcoming tournament. Play the front nine or back nine of the course you will be competing on. Picture the holes you will be playing and strive to hit its fairways and greens. Once complete, go back to the beginning, and try again with the aim of beating your initial score.

The Inner Workings of Skills Tests

You now have a few examples of the type of skills tests that Hugh and I would like you to complete. If you commit to this type of practice you will build a greater understanding of your game, you will build skill, and you will improve.

Of course there are some rules and guidelines to adhere to if you want to get the most from your skills testing. Here are some inner workings of this vital practice.

Estimation

Many of you reading this book won't have the facilities to measure skills tests accurately. You may not be able to mark out distances and radiuses. That's fine. You will have to estimate measurements, but that alone is better than not doing skills tests at all.

Don't make your facilities your excuse. Your game is too important for that. Skills tests have too much of an impact to brush them aside simply because you have to use a little more imagination to put them into practice.

Set Targets Low, then Progress

Set your measurement parameters based on your experience, ability and competence. It's an obvious statement to make, but the better the player you are - the tougher you should make your tests. Let me give you an example.

The test 'Off the Tee' can be varied according to who is playing the game. Better players may start with a fairway 20 yards wide then re-test with a fairway 15 yards wide. Those who want to re-create the conditions of the 1999 British Open at Carnoustie may wish to try and hit to a fairway 10 yards in width!

The reverse is true as well. Recreational golfers of modest ability could set themselves a wide fairway of 40 yards. They could also set themselves a more modest target of hitting 50% onto the cut stuff. The great thing about all skills tests is that progression can be seen easily.

Practice requires a purpose. Always work towards being slightly better in every training session.

Work on Mindset

This book is going to be packed with ideas on how to manage your mind. Whether it's maintaining a positive approach, staying in control of emotions, or dealing with distractions - the answers can be found in the remaining chapters.

Skills tests are a fantastic platform to challenge your ability to stay in control of your mindset. If you're on a bad run of shots - work on keeping yourself calm. If your mind is wandering or distracted every few minutes, take appropriate action to retain your focus. If your confidence is sapped from a few bad shots use the examples from this book to give yourself a boost of positivity.

As Hugh Marr would say, skills tests are your stress tests. They are powerful game changers because they create a practice environment that incorporates the kind of pressure you'll experience out on the course in a competition. By testing your skills you are training the interaction between the physical side of the game and the mental side of golf.

Test and Re-test, then Keep a Record

The essence of testing is in the re-testing. Doing a skills test once will focus your mind for half an hour but it won't give your brain a blast of certainty or a hit of confidence. Make sure you are re-testing on a regular basis and keep a record of your scores. You want to see progression, but regression is useful too. Progression demonstrates an improvement in your skill set, while regressive scores should signal a trip to your coach. Uncovering what you have to work on to improve your skills test scores is your next port of call.

Give your skills test scores to your coach. Take him through the testing procedures if he is unaware of the games you are playing. More feedback for him helps diagnosis – data gives him a sense of where you are with your game, the mistakes you are making, as well as an awareness of the bad habits and patterns that are creeping into your game.

Align with Lessons and Learn as you Progress

If you've recently had a lesson on putting then it would be wasteful to head straight out onto the range to complete a long game skills test. Whilst a golfer should complete a mix of tests each month I would advise you to emphasise those that are *most relevant* to the lesson you've just had.

Avoid being too passive as you work through the tests. Certainly steer clear of a 'going through the motions' state of mind. Engage in the learning process. The outcome of testing is mediated by your focus and by the effort you put in. Pay full attention and go through the shot routine you'll learn in the 'prepare' section of this book. By taking each shot seriously you mirror the competition intensity you demonstrate when you play in a monthly medal, matchplay event, or local tournament. Be intentional and engage with the right intensity.

Create your Own Tests

Finally, and perhaps most importantly, create your own tests. Use your imagination. If you take a little time to think about it, and put your mind to it, your own creations will be better and more relevant for you than any test set by someone else.

For those who are super keen - keep a folder of tests and a notebook to record your scores. Also jot down your thoughts behind both good and bad test results. Observation committed to paper will linger in the mind longer and speed your progress towards Golf Tough.

The more you test yourself, the better you'll be when you play in testing conditions.

The Sweet Sound of Skill

Ultimately when you face down a 165 yard approach shot to a tight green or a tricky chip with the green sloping away from you it feels good to *know* - to *know* you've been there before. You want a brain primed to react with confidence. You want a pressure-proofed brain.

Skills testing is a critical essential. A golf brain that has seen it before, done it before, and executed under pressure is one that is ready for competitive action. As a practice protocol it enunciates stress and places burden on your confidence. It helps you practice Golf Tough.

Enriching your practice ground habits is a Golf Tough must. It takes focus and commitment, but its rewards are great.

I'd like you to construct a practice schedule that both Hugh and I would be proud of. I'd like you to get down and dirty with your skill development. Experiment! Test yourself. Set up a little adversity and strive to build a mind that copes effectively with pressure. Next time you're at the range perhaps take a little time to ask yourself "What would Hugh say?" Would you impress a hard-to-please Scotsman, or would you incur his wrath? He has, after all, flown in to see you.

In golf, head and heart are inextricably linked. Skills testing is the domain of the intelligent player, the one who wants to be Golf Tough. But intelligent players must also have the heart to exploit the brain that drives their hands. Practicing in the way Hugh Marr wants you to practice is challenging. In fact, practicing in the way all world class coaches want you to practice is challenging. It's not the same as beating a bucket of balls. If you prefer the latter I don't blame you. It's the road more travelled and the path of ease. But if you're still with the elite, and you fancy staying the course, then the next chapter will compliment Hugh's methodology.

3

Tuning Your Golf Engine

Allow me to regale you with an 'X-Factor' piece of research from the annals of academic psychology. The results of this study are exciting – seriously groundbreaking. Perhaps they should be accompanied with a victory warning – 'serious success guaranteed'. I promise you, given the outcomes the study found, if you commit to its wisdom you'll give yourself a great chance to achieve just about anything you set out to accomplish. That sounds good, right? So let me tell you this secret to success; you're not going to be disappointed.

In 1953, graduates of Yale University were surveyed to determine how many of them had specific, written goals for their future. The answer was a paltry 3%. A tiny minority of students had bothered to sit down and articulate, on paper, exactly what they wanted to achieve in life. This small group had carved out their future story in detail. Some wanted to be doctors, others wanted to make a living from the law, whilst some wanted to go into banking. In contrast a whopping 97% of the graduate students only had a vague idea of what their future lives looked like. Crucially they had failed to compose a written list of their prospective occupations.

Twenty years later, researchers polled the surviving members of the Class of 1953 and found some amazing results - the 3% with goals had accumulated more personal financial wealth than the other 97% of the class combined! So there we have it. Research has shown that if you don't write out your goals you'll give yourself less chance of succeeding in life. Incredible!

Incredible, but not true. This neat little anecdote that has been told the world over by self-help gurus on stage, and in many of their books, is completely made up. An exhaustive investigation by Yale uncovered no longitudinal research at all. They believe no study took place. They believe it is a myth.

I have started this chapter with a parable on goal setting not because I want to talk to you about setting targets for your game, but because golf, like many things in life has been subject to untruths, fabricated 'facts', and falsehoods that have become a part of the golfing language and entrenched into the belief system of golfers. Allow me to give you a few examples.

How often do we hear people respond to a topped shot with a cry of "Keep your head down"? Well, from the conversations I've had with PGA professional coaches, it probably isn't the lifting of your head that caused you to top the ball. Apparently there are many causes for a topped shot. In fact, I've been told that trying to keep your 'head down' *prevents* you from swinging freely through the ball. Keeping your head down tends to *cause* bad shots rather than avoid them. And yet this piece of technical advice has become a part of golfing 'wisdom'. And it's a lore that has stuck and probably won't be going away very soon.

My next example brings me to the crux of this chapter. Being a sport psychologist you may be surprised to hear my next eulogy.

The Deniable Truth about Golf

I believe, with all my heart, that golf is a game of mindset. But I also *know* that it is a game of technique. It's a game of turn and hinge, shift and release. It's a game of alignment, aim and posture. I also think it is a game of physicality. It's a game of strength and power, movement and flexibility.

I say this because, as a sport psychologist, I don't believe in the notion that golf is 90% or 80% or even 70% mental. I don't believe that the mind can cure a slice or heal a hook. I don't believe that you can will the ball into the hole. I don't believe that good thinking alone can turn you into a scratch golfer. I don't believe you can listen to a positive thinking MP3 every day and go shoot under par when 85 is your normal number. I don't believe it is the mind alone that rips the ball down the middle of the fairway. I don't do pseudo-science and I don't do pop psychology.

But I *do* believe that when a golfer commits himself to training his mind then he will positively impact his game in a profound way. I *do* believe a 90 shooter can break into the 80's. I *do* believe an 80's player can hit the 70's. I *do* believe that a scratch golfer can shoot in the 60's on a regular basis. And I do believe these kinds of shifts can be a product of an improvement in mindset. But your mind's impact on your golf game comes with limitations. There are boundaries set by logic, reason and scientific principles.

To quote John Jacobs, one of the greatest golf instructors of all time: "Golf is what the ball does and what the ball does is determined by what the clubhead tells it to do." What the clubhead does is primarily influenced by the pattern of your body movements. Sure, how you think, what you are focusing on, and the level of your confidence, all mediate how the club is delivered onto the ball and this is the message of this book and, for that matter, most books on sport psychology. But more immediately it is your hands and arms, your torso and legs, which influence the motion of the clubhead.

Golf is what the ball does and what the ball does is determined by what the clubhead tells it to do. With this mantra in mind I would argue that the engine room of your golf game is not your brain but your body. It is not your mind but your swing. Let's look at your engine a little closer.

Tuning Your Golf Engine

Maybe yours looks a little like Phil's? Maybe yours is long and languid with an air of smoothness but a release with bullet speed.

In contrast, maybe yours is a little like Jim's? Maybe yours is idiosyncratic and peculiar but effective.

Or perhaps yours is like Luke's? Maybe yours is aesthetically pleasing, and geared for accuracy rather than length.

Maybe yours doesn't look like Mickelson's, Furyk's or Donald's, and it probably doesn't function like their swings either. But whatever it looks like - your swing is your golf engine. Everyone's is a little different in style and, even at the top level of the game, there are few commonalities between players' motions. The fact remains, however, *your swing is your engine*.

Section 1 | Chapter 3

Despite the aesthetic and technical differences between the swings on the world's professional Tours they all have a commonality. They are all effective. Every player making a living from playing the game returns the clubhead back to the ball in a manner that creates highly consistent outcomes. All of these players are technically sound. They are playing for mega bucks because their swings work optimally for them.

There is no getting away from it – you need a swing that works. Thinking differently isn't going to help you put on 20 yards of length. Better focus isn't going to help you go from hitting an average of 6 greens in regulation, per round, to an average of 12. If you, more often than not, fail to get the ball out of the bunker, a shift of belief isn't going to see you zip the ball out to 3 feet from the greenside trap 80% of the time.

A mentally tough golfer who swings too steeply into the ball or leaves his clubhead trailing his body through impact won't rip the flag out – he'll spray shots left and right. Mindset can influence and manage the effects of physics but it cannot *override* force, energy and motion.

Having a great mentality on the course will help you swing the club, and stroke the ball, to the very best of your ability - that is all. But please bear with me. The mental side of golf encompasses so much more than on-course play. Your engine – your swing – is heavily influenced by psychology in ways that, at first glance, are less than obvious.

Not only does mindset play a part in the execution of your swing, it is also involved in the tuning of your golf engine. To be Golf Tough you need to develop a process of improving your swing. And this is when your brain needs full engagement.

Your body is the engine of your golf. But it's your mind that supercharges your engine!

The Undeniable Truth about Mindset and Technique

Picture some of the greatest golf champions practicing - the hardest workers. Nick Faldo changing his swing in the late 1980's. Tiger going through the three famous changes he's made to his technique. Vijay Singh rifling ball after ball into the Floridian sun. Ben Hogan, a solitary figure in Fort Worth, finding the sweetspot time and time again. Gary Player, getting luckier the harder he worked. Jack Nicklaus as a kid, ripping 200 of the little suckers down the range – everyday!

Champions work at their swing through searing heat. They drill and repeat, drill and repeat through rain and wind, sometimes in snow. They always have done and they always will. Why would the weather matter when their eyes are fixed firmly on the prize? Motivation, the Gore-Tex of distraction!

Try to put yourself in their minds. Slide into their thoughts. That intensity! That relentless march towards the unobtainable - perfection. Uncompromising! No doubts – just a vision of how they want their swing to be. Nothing to the left, no sight to the right. Just them, their clubs, the balls, their motion, their mechanics, and up ahead a cluster of balls on the fairway.

What do the golfing greats have in common? Sure, they're all talented. They all have above average hand-eye coordination. And hard work is their maxim. They have all wiled away hours on the practice ground, on the pitching area and the putting green honing their game. But with every champion there is something less ordinary sizzling away.

To my mind it is the subtle art of *learning* that so often differentiates in sport. The ability to learn separates one golfer from another. It separates their speed of improvement, the ceiling of their handicap and their range of shots. Of course talent - your in-born capability - makes a difference. Science has repeatedly demonstrated that people learn at different rates depending on the make-up of their nervous system. But the exciting thing is that *anyone* can enrich their ability to learn. Anyone can quicken their rate of improvement.

Golf is what the ball does, and what the ball does is determined by what the clubhead tells it to do. Technique is the engine of your golf game, but technique is underpinned by your psychology – by your mindset on the course and, just as emphatically, by your ability to learn. The golfing greats are great learners - they have a mind to learn. When they take time to improve their technique they don't just beat balls, they are engrossed in the moment and immerse themselves in the movement they want. They are focused on making *connections*.

Super Charging your Engine

There are trillions of tiny connections between the cells in your brain that make you the person you are. These connections inform your behaviour, they determine how you think, and they shape your life. Each time you learn something new you activate different brain cells and create new connections between cells. For example, cells have wired together for the time you have been playing golf to enable you to swing the way you do and putt the way you putt - the internal structure of your brain is a physical representation of your golfing ability. Your golf brain is your golf game! When you learn a new swing technique you create new connections – your brain literally changes its structure.

This process gets to the heart of growth. Your brain wiring is powerful. There are more connections in your brain than there are stars in the universe. Information crosses these connections at approximately 268 miles per hour allowing us to think and act effectively, and move and behave appropriately. Improving and developing your golf game is a simple process of creating new connections between cells in your brain. And what we now know in brain science is that the brain can continue to establish new connections (and learn) for the whole of your life. It may be easier to learn when you're younger but it's still very possible to keep learning throughout the whole of adulthood. Thus, no matter what your age, you *can* improve your swing. You *can* ingrain new movement and technique.

There is a useful 'road' analogy I use with golfers to explain this brain wiring process. When you start learning a new technique the connections between cells are small and weak. At this stage you are building pathways (think of a simple, scraggy old country pathway). Signals between cells at this stage are slow (after all you can't race a car down a pathway, you can only stroll down one). Executing the new technique is challenging - you have to really think about what you're doing as you're doing it. After a little bit of practice your pathways start to become stronger and roads start to form. Signals become more powerful and speed up. Your technique starts to evolve – it feels more natural and more comfortable. You no longer feel like you've been asked to write with your weaker hand.

As you continue to practice, your new technique becomes commonplace in your swing or stroke. It can be executed smoothly, efficiently and effectively. At this stage you've turned the roads into motorways. Connections are stronger (think of the reinforcement of a motorway) and quicker (think of the higher speed limit on a highway).

The champions of golf are the ones who have race tracks in their brain. Their levels of practice have developed connections that are thick and insulated and the speed with which messages travel across brain cells is rapid. They have these speedy connections for every part of their game – putting, chipping, pitching, and the long game. This is why their bodies move in perfect harmony with the club. This is how they make the complex look simple.

I love this analogy because, to my mind, not only does it demystify the art of learning, it also presents the possibility of improvement. I abhor the notion that my skillset will stay static forever. I want to go on learning, developing and improving. And the neurological evidence I have presented to you, above, albeit simplistic, helps me to believe I can turn that ambition into reality. You *can* become better technically with your swing. You *can* become better technically with your pitching. You *can* improve your putting stroke. An old dog can *always* learn new tricks!

But just because you 'can' doesn't mean that it's easy. Don't let my simple driving analogy fool you into thinking it will be. Turning paths into race tracks requires more than just hard work. Some say repetition is the mother of skill. I say repetition is only its potential parent. It is the *quality* of your practice more so than the quantity that establishes keen connections between cells. Quality, focused practice makes brain cells hungry to connect. An hour of engaged practice will shape your game quicker and more effectively than three hours of inattentive training will do.

Let's take a closer look at quality practice and begin to turn paths into roads.

It is quality more than quantity of practice that delivers excellence in golf. Practice with a focused, goal driven mind.

Focus – Pathways into Roads

Your journey to technical excellence begins here. You have something to change and this is the start line. Maybe you need to turn your body rather than move laterally on the backswing. Maybe you need to shift your weight to the front foot on the downswing and into the followthrough. Whatever your next technical challenge you're going to deal with it head on, with intelligence and with the learning brain in mind.

The correct focus is our first pit stop to soup up your golfing engine. Without focus you cannot create connections. *With* focus we start to mould our roads from pathways. Here we give our brain a platform to build connections – lots of them, functioning at super speed.

The first rule of focused learning is simple - *distractions prevent connections.*

A wandering mind cannot shape the brain for excellence. A dispersed focus cannot shape a brain primed for technical brilliance. Let's use a common example to illustrate.

You have recently had a lesson where your coach has adjusted your takeaway. Rather than allowing you to stick with the wristy move away from the ball that you've had over the past few years, your coach wants you to ingrain more of a one piece motion. This action will help you to achieve some width in the backswing, not only helping shallow your angle of attack into the ball (building consistency of strike) but also helping you apply more force into the ball. You'll be able to hit it further.

Now you have the information it's time to head down to the range and build some new connections and some messaging speed across the brain. It's time to turn pathways into roads.

Get yourself 50 balls. Don't purchase the big bucket – there are too many balls and you'll never focus in an effective manner. Too many balls is counterintuitive. 50 is enough.

To build roads you need to immerse yourself in the process of swing change. Allow your focus to be absorbed, in the moment, on the movement that needs adjusting. Did Ben Hogan look up to watch what others were doing? He was too busy building roads. Did Jack Nicklaus place his attention on anything other than his swing? He was too busy building roads. If distraction disperses your attention bring it back to your swing as quickly as possible. The quicker you do so the less distraction bites.

The second rule of learning is, again, simple. *Outcomes prevent connections.*

When great golfers strive to develop their technique they focus on either their body or the club or both. They avoid focusing on the outcome of shots. This may seem like a foreign idea to you but, remember, when working your technique you are not trying to get an immediate change of ball flight, you are trying to change the motion of your swing. Outcome is, for the time being, irrelevant.

There is another reason why a golfer who is trying to change technique should avoid observing the outcome of the shots she is hitting. Outcome can awaken negative emotions and trigger tightness in the body. When you hit several shots, that you judge as poor, you can increase your levels of anxiety and worry. Your internal voice may resonate with doubt at the changes you are making. In turn your physical body may quietly and subtly adjust, with your shoulders stiffening and your hands tensing up.

These psychological and physical changes add many hours to the amount of practice you have to complete in order to ingrain a new technical habit. With one exception (which I will outline below) I would avoid taking notice of where the ball flies as you hit balls for technical change. Having the attitude that 'the ball just gets in the way' will help you stay relaxed and engaged on the task at hand.

Focus is a choice – you get to choose in what direction it travels.

Intensity and Interest – Roads into Motorways

The third rule of learning (which is a close relative of the first rule) – *boredom prevents connections*.

The intensity of your practice begins with a choice. You can choose to become captivated by the motion of your swing or you can choose to scatter your energy onto other things and let your mind wander. As outlined above, the simple process of noticing when your focus has shifted and your intensity has dropped can help you to return your mindset back to your swing.

Thankfully there are ways you can deliberately maintain your intensity and subsequent focus as you practice. My first suggestion is to be absolutely clear how long you are going to practice for, and to make a mental commitment that you will maintain the quality of your session for the allotted period. The brain craves certainty, so give it a dose of assurance. By giving yourself a direct instruction, such as "I will practice for 50 balls" or "I will practice for one hour" you lock in the behaviours you require to practice your game in the most effective way.

A technique to help absorb the mind in the moment, and one that is popular amongst my clients, involves asking yourself questions as you practice.

- "Did I keep my takeaway in one piece on that swing?"
- "How did that move feel when compared to the last swing?"
- "On a scale of 0-10 what would I give myself for that swing execution?"
- "What can I do differently to give myself a higher score out of 10?"

Great questions pique your interest levels. They help place your attention in the moment and on the specific swing challenge that confronts you. They help you reflect after every shot and appraise the quality of the swing you made.

A final idea that will help you turn pathways into roads may seem a contradiction to my belief that to develop technique a golfer should ignore the outcome of his shots. But hear me out.

If your coach wants you to work on an area of your swing to cure a certain shape of shot then it is likely he will help you ingrain a move that initially causes the opposite ball flight to happen. For example, if you slice the ball, your coach may work on helping you develop a swing path that makes it more likely for you to hook or draw the ball. Similarly, if you tend to balloon the ball high your coach may work with you to lower your trajectory. A new move in your swing may see you hit the ball very low – the complete opposite of what you were doing before.

In this circumstance paying attention to your ball flight can prove a useful platform to change your swing *and* maintain your interest levels. A slicer might try and hit 10 hooks in a row. A natural fader of the ball who wants to straighten up his drives could try and hit 5 draws in a row.

Sometimes, when boredom sets in, it's useful to vary where you place your focus. I strongly advise that for the most part, say 75% of the time, it is more adaptive to ignore ball flight. But if you feel a little jaded and need an injection of interest then start observing the ball flight. Set yourself some challenges, but always relate the ball flight back to the swing move you are trying to change or develop.

A Sensory Blast – Motorways into Race Tracks

Take your time as you practice. Allow your brain a brief moment to absorb the swing you've just made. Avoid scraping in the next ball. Imagine your brain as a 'Word document' with every shot a different paragraph that needs saving.

The time in-between shots is so important. It's where the real learning takes place. It's where motorways become race tracks. It's when the brain soaks up the information from a swing so it can repeat it correctly the next time.

It's also a time when you can take direct control of the input into your brain. You can do this by taking plenty of practice swings. Take them at full pace and at half pace. Reduce them to slow motion so your brain gets a rich kinaesthetic snapshot of the motion you want to ingrain.

Feel the swing you want to make time and time again. Place all your energy and focus onto executing the new movement, if not with perfection at least with excellence. Turning motorways into race tracks requires precision.

Incorporate a sensory blast into your practice swings. Feel the swing you want to make, feel a great strike on the ball and as you swing through - see the shot fly away on the perfect trajectory. Feel it, hear it, and see it.

Don't be afraid to do this in your mind. In psychology we call this 'imagery' or 'visualisation'. Take your stance and, without moving, feel yourself move the club away from the ball. Travel through your swing in your mind without stopping. Make sure you click into that perfect swing mode, really see it – if you can't get it right in your head you won't get it right for real.

This process works because the brain can't tell the difference between what is real and what is imagined. What we now know in science is that when you imagine yourself swinging a club your brain cells fire. There's even evidence to suggest that the cells start to connect up – just by imagining the movement we want.

Whether the science community discover this to be 100% accurate or not, it is without question a worthwhile process. Taking sensory rich practice swings helps create a blueprint for your brain that you can then re-create when you swing for real. Using imagery when standing over the ball adds that sense of realism that boosts your ability to turn motorways into high speed race tracks.

This isn't groundbreaking stuff. Open up any book on sport psychology and you'll read about the importance of imagery and visualisation. But despite its mainstream popularity very few people actually use their senses in a practical way. It certainly isn't commonplace on the driving range. I rarely see golfers take time between shots to practice their swing physically or mentally. Of course I can't *see* whether golfers practice their swing mentally, but it doesn't take a psychic to know that the beat balls mentality probably doesn't fit with the feel it, hear it, see it process that enriches the learning experience.

Golfing race tracks crafted in your brain are not as a result of simply 'doing'. They are the end result of doing *and* thinking. Great practice incorporates swing and think, think and swing. That process produces a deeper more meaningful method of learning. It produces a powerful engine room. Perhaps even a Grand Prix engine.

Using your senses as you train, as you practice, leads to a deeper, richer form of learning.

Your Grand Prix Engine

Your experiences in life sculpt the connections in your brain. So do your experiences in golf. This is how I like my clients to think of practice - an experience.

Make sure your practice experiences are rich and big and bold and bright. Focus through them. Make repetition an important behaviour, but make your positive practice attitude an indispensable must. The owner of a Grand Prix engine emphasises quality over quantity at every pit stop.

Whether it's skill development through skills testing or whether it's technical practice you are committed to, your sessions carve paths into your brain wiring and shape your golf game. Those who practice Golf Tough give themselves a chance to play Golf Tough. But there's another component to consider before a game of Golf Tough is possible. Great golfers prepare with precision. You need world class preparation. We will summarise this section first and then go and learn about world class preparation.

Driving Your Golf Tough Practice

Chapter One

1. Commit to recording your golf statistics.
2. Work with a PGA Golf Professional to interpret your data.
3. Build your confidence as you see your numbers improve.

Chapter Two

1. Know the difference between technique and skill.
2. Engage in skills tests.
3. Make your skills tests competitive – test and re-test.

Chapter Three

1. Recognise that technique is the engine room of your golf game.
2. Learning a new technique is heavily influenced by mindset.
3. Put quality over quantity in your technical practice.

4

Finding Your Game Face

It was a swinging fifteen foot putt that won it for him. The ball had snaked its way down the lightning quick 18th green at Augusta and disappeared into the left edge of the hole. The patrons had whooped and hollered for one of their own and he himself had leapt with joy. A hug for caddie Jim 'Bones' Mackay and a kiss for the ball that had changed his world - Phil Mickelson, the All American kid, had finally won. He had endured 15 years of hurt as a professional - 15 Majorless years for the golfing phenomenon from California – but now that hurt had dissolved amid a back nine from heaven.

He had led the pack in many PGA Tour events – he had even won one as an amateur. He knew how to win those. But after a decade, followed by five years as a pro, one of the big four had eluded him. Agonisingly beaten by the late great Payne Stewart at Merion in '99, and close shaves elsewhere with five other top 3 finishes, in four consecutive years, until 2003 - had done little to temper his desire to win on Major Sunday. But the 2004 Masters had set the scene for a different Mickelson – one more at ease with his surroundings. Something inside him had stirred:

"I had a different feeling playing this week. I had a different feeling entering this tournament. I just had a real belief that I was going to come through this week."

And he had *refused* to let that belief waver. He had *refused* to allow the course or the situation to break the feelings of belief that had gripped his body.

"I kept saying to myself over and over 'This is my day, this is my day'."

Mickelson had been a mammoth three shots behind the multiple major champion Ernie Els standing on the 12th tee and yet he continued his positive mantra:

"This is my day, this is my day."

He birdied 12. He knew he had opportunities up ahead and he didn't ignore this fact - he quietly reminded himself of the par 5's, the 13th and 15th holes. For him ignoring the score wasn't important – he wanted to embrace the fact that he had birdie chances close by. His mindset feasted on the fact that his long shots could eat up the reachable 5's. He proceeded to birdie 13 and then stuck his approach to within a couple of inches of the flag on 14. He was still behind but he allowed a smile to envelope his face at this mini success. He was going to stay relentless – he wasn't going to stop the self-talk that was driving him on:

"This is my day, this is my day."

Led by his inner voice, his positive feelings continued to resonate throughout his body. That surge of belief shot through his swing on the short 16th. Pin back left he fired for the middle of the green knowing that a straight hit would feed down the green for a flattish putt. A strong release through impact and the ball behaved nicely – it did exactly what he had envisioned. A twenty footer later and he was tied for the lead. He made a safe par down 17 and then two ripped shots to the green on 18 left him with *that* fifteen foot putt - the only shot left between him and Major success.

Mickelson was in a different mindset on that balmy evening back in 2004. He was in a different frame of mind. He was in control. He was thinking clearly and he was feeling confident. He had his game face on and he was Golf Tough.

Your Game Face

We can still see it in him now. It's there whenever he plays a major. That slow, relaxed lolloping walk. That semi-smile that rarely shifts. A focused face, wide eyed. That kid-like attitude influenced by the love of play. The small but gracious head nod to acknowledge the crowd. A long wristy swing, a powerful ball flight, a silky smooth stroke on the cut stuff and a delicate touch around the green. Phil Mickelson has a game face and he carries it with him wherever he plays.

All champions do. Muhammad Ali's brash arrogance, Michael Jordan's focus, Michael Phelps's unrelenting toughness. All champions have a game face. All champions have a style, a formula of how to be, how to think, how to act, how to feel and how to behave. It's the ingredients that mix the cocktail of their game. It's their prescription when they're down, one that can be summoned even in the depths of despair. And it drives their performance under pressure, helping them hold their nerve as stress bears down on the final few holes.

Let me be clear. A game face isn't just a facial expression. It incorporates both body and mind. It's physical as well as psychological. It's a way of holding yourself and a way of being. It's an outward projection of an inner attitude that can be seen from head to toe.

A champion's game face is always close by. It is a part of him or her just as *your* game face is a part of *you*. Its origins lie hidden in the depths of your personality but rise everyday to the surface of your behaviour – it is not completely invisible nor out of reach. Allow me to explain the source of your game face further by planting an image in your mind. Think of your favourite golfer. Fix a picture of him or her and hold it for a while. Think of them swinging the club – their set up, backswing and followthrough. Now let your mind wander away from their swing onto their body language. How do they hold themselves? How do they walk? How do they talk? Home in on the detail and look for clues of their game face. It's there in every play they take, every gesture they make, every moment of every round. Before we take an in depth exploration of yours, let's look at a couple of famous ones.

Knowing your game face is powerful. It's as important as having a solid putting stroke and a smooth swing.

Tiger's Eyes

Tiger prowls. He strides with confidence. A pace with quick tempo - one to match his swing. He walks quickly with not much conversation – a mind on his job, a mind on effort. When his strike is off, or his flight is poor, anger engulfs him – the perfectionist personified. But such is his will to win, the anger that tears through his body soon dissipates and his volume of focus increases - ready to execute the next shot. Calm once again. In control!

A competitor! Every shot struck with attention to detail. Every putt read with focus vibrating across his mind and belief coursing through his body. A never give in attitude! Perfectly executed routines delivered regardless of his score, position or status in the tournament.

That is the Tiger Woods we know and that is the Tiger Woods we love to watch. He is as unique a golfer as you are. His game face is his and his alone. A man known for his mental toughness, his fortitude and resilience; perhaps one of the differences that makes Tiger the golfer he is lies in the fact that he knows his game face. He doesn't guess his success formula – he pays attention to his personality and his preferred style. He doesn't take who he is for granted - he uses the best of himself as he competes, no matter the score, no matter the round, no matter the tournament.

The Big Easy

The Big Easy has a different game face. It strikes a different beat. Like his swing it's slow and smooth. It's quiet but steely determined. It's calm and serene. It fronts a relaxed body, but don't let his exterior deceive you. He may have a mind made of ice, but he has a fire alight in his belly. His desire to win equals any game hungry professional.

Ernie Els is something else. He moves his 6'3" frame through 18 holes in an imposing but tranquil manner. He is the winner of four Majors not only because of his prodigious talent, but also because he knows his best thoughts and his optimum behaviours – the ones that give him the best chance to make birdies and keep bogeys off the card. He knows what to do if he hits a bad shot, makes a double bogey or misses a short putt. He knows how to express himself and how to hold himself when opportunity is lost.

Tiger and Ernie – two champions with contrasting features. Two different game faces. Knowing your game face and applying it on the course in competition golf is half the battle won.

Know yourself... Know you at your Best... and Repeat!

Let me give you a piece of common sense that is, in my opinion, uncommonly executed - do what you do, and think how you think, when you are at your very best - then repeat relentlessly.

That is what champions do. That is what the best golfers, athletes, boxers, tennis players and footballers do. They repeat the recipe that drives their personal success time and again. That is their secret formula and it should be *yours*. That is *your* path to consistency.

But this isn't what most golfers do. Most golfers play without a sense of the thoughts, feelings and behaviours they have when they play at their best. They aren't aware of what they tend to focus on when they shoot under their handicap. They remain blissfully ignorant of the mindset and physical state that helps them make birdies, hole putts, and stiff approach shots.

Many of the answers you need to play Golf Tough are already inside of you. You may not be aware of them right now but the clues are there to be unravelled. You simply need to bring to the surface *who* you are as a golfer, *what* you do when you play at your best - and then repeat, repeat, repeat!

I'd like you to start thinking about you at your very best now. I'd like you to dwell on your greatest rounds of golf or set of holes. We're going to use some of the images you are currently summoning up later in this chapter.

One of the first questions I ask a golf client, whether we're standing on the range, walking the course or sitting with a beer in the nineteenth is: "Tell me about your best golf." This isn't because I want my pupil to ignore her weaknesses - it's more because I want to orientate her towards the patterns of thinking and behaviours that she executes when she plays at 10/10, or close to her own definition of excellence.

I want her mind re-living her best because I know this is the template we are going to use for her game face. I want her to become addicted to her most accomplished habits. And I want *you* to experience the same thing. I want you to re-live and replay your most proficient performances on the golf course. Once you've stencilled this into your mind you have a powerful model to reinforce daily, and repeat relentlessly, come tournament or medal day.

It is important, if not imperative, for you to become a strengths-based golfer. This is how Golf Tough is done. And this approach is widely supported by evidence from the worlds of psychotherapy and change management.

Champions dwell on their best every day. They immerse themselves in their success formulas on and off the course.

A Strength-Based, Solution-Oriented Approach

Golfers who want to play Golf Tough need to do more of what works and less of what doesn't. By and large, golfers aren't great at doing this. If they play well they celebrate with a drink in the nineteenth with friends, but they don't necessarily take time to recollect, in detail, the thoughts, feelings, actions and behaviours that helped them to shoot low. In contrast, poor performances tend to be mentally bookmarked. A bad round is followed by a commiseration in the bar and a discussion of the worst moments. The missed putt is replayed endlessly and the bad thinking on the final tee is talked about relentlessly.

Because of this 'negative' phenomenon, golfers lean towards being brilliant at remembering and repeating what *doesn't* work for them, and lousy at remembering and repeating what *does* work. We, as golfers, need the reverse. If you want to develop an outstanding game face you need to know what *does* work.

Some of the most effective therapies that aid those engulfed in depression, alcoholism and other clinical challenges take this 'do more of what works, and less of what doesn't work' route to affecting change. For example, therapists who use a model called *Solution Focus Brief Therapy* help patients re-live the moments when their problems aren't there. They ask alcoholics to talk through times when they *don't* want a drink. And they discuss with depressed patients the periods when they *don't* feel depressed. Therapists then help patients look for clues – actions, behaviours, mannerisms and ways of thinking – that are part of these periods, when the clinical issue isn't present. These clues help the therapist and patient build solutions to combat the compulsion to drink or the likelihood of falling into a depression. Do what you do, or think how you think, when you are not drinking or when you are not depressed – an elegant and simple approach to helping people manage their challenges.

This approach can also be used effectively in the world of sport. The game of the tennis player who has come off the court playing his best, most outstanding tennis, leaves clues to be uncovered and repeated. The match of the soccer player which has seen him score a hat-trick and bamboozle the defence with incredible movement and electric pace leaves clues to be unearthed and replicated.

Your game face is, quite simply, *you* – the personality you bring to the golf course and the thoughts, feelings, actions and behaviours when you play your very best golf. Let's reveal what your game face looks like.

Never forget your best rounds. Great golf leaves clues behind that you can use again and again.

Your Game Face Plays

I'd like you to sit back and think about your golf. I want you to take some time to envision the golf you play when you're at your very best. Pick a competitive round in living memory when you experienced your finest golf. It matters little what your handicap is or how long you have been playing. It's not relevant what course you play, how often you get the sticks out, or what make of clubs you use. We all have a personal blueprint of us at our very best on the course.

Start to build a video in your mind. What does it look like? What does it feel like? Make your inner pictures high definition.

Take some time to study yourself from the outside in. Peer at yourself from the side of the fairway. Notice your movement. What is it like? How do you hold yourself? In what style are you walking? Are you quick or slow? Are you upbeat or downbeat? Would you describe yourself as energetic or relaxed? Now watch yourself swing - is your tempo slow or is it fast?

To open a few more inner pictures for you, let me give you a comparison with two professionals, ones we have already mentioned. When you play are you more Tiger Woods or Ernie Els? Are you a fiery character or do you lean more towards a chilled out temperament? Do you walk at a quick pace between shots or are you more of a stroller?

Then take a little time to reflect on the inside out. What are you thinking as you play at your best? What are you saying to yourself? How are you feeling? What bodily sensations are you experiencing as you compete at your best?

Allow your high performance thoughts and feelings to resonate. Not only do you want to take a snapshot of the actions you take when you play at your best, you also want to press record on the *inner voice* you enjoy as you compete. Multiply the experience by thinking about the feelings you experienced as you stride the fairways and greens.

If you struggle to think of a whole round then choose a stretch of holes that you have been particularly pleased with in the past. Nominating a front or back 9 when you played your personal form of incredible golf – that stretch when nothing could go wrong - is a useful memory to grab hold of.

Now I'd like you to associate some words to the internal pictures you are creating and some phrases that describe you at your best. Here are some that my clients have chosen recently:

- "Confident and tall"
- "Staying patient"
- "Bold, aggressive and upbeat"
- "Complete commitment"
- "Immersed in my routine, one shot at a time"
- "Slow with belief"
- "Smooth with constant breaths"
- "Relaxed but strong – big player in the group"
- "Unrelenting focus by the ball, relaxed down the fairway"
- "Fun and freedom"

Your game face should be full of magical statements that stand out - that resonate big and bold and bright images in you. When you think about them you should be able to see the exact actions and the precise processes that they encapsulate. They should send a wave of confidence and a hit of belief through your body. They should excite you, they should focus your mind and they should push doubts, worries and anxieties to the side – at least temporarily. Let's give you some more of my clients' game face plays:

- "Only focus on me"
- "Upbeat on the tee and on the green"
- "Quick pace, slow routine"
- "Athletic over the ball"
- "Dial in with wedges – dominate the pin"
- "Be relentless with my mindset"
- "Slow after bad shots, slow after great shots"
- "Powerful walk, athletic swing"
- "Chatty and relaxed... play my game"
- "Exact yardages – then trust my swing"

The plays in your game face should be a mix of descriptions related to actions and thoughts. After all, you need to be able to go and re-create them. They should also incorporate a blend of images allied with intelligent and emotional golf. Great performances in sport are shot through with emotion. You need evocative words and phrases - emotional words tend to puncture our mindset and help us climb into that all important 'ready to go' state of mind.

There are hundreds of game face plays to choose from. But your choices must be meaningful to *you*. They aren't the game face representations of Tiger Woods or Ernie Els or Rory McIlroy. They are *your* plays. This is *your* script, no-one else's.

I would like you to come up with between three and five plays. Any less and you haven't discovered the heart of your best golf – you will need to work on your self-awareness. Any more and you'll make your game face too complex and too overwhelming. In golf, simplicity offers the elegant solution!

Now get your game face plays written down (or at least lodged firmly in your mind) – I have another question for you.

Your Intensity Sweet Spot

Let's take a scale from 0 to 10. 0 represents your intensity levels when you are asleep, while 10 is more towards a highly strung, highly emotional, headless chicken persona.

Think about executing your game face plays – the words and phrases that represent your key thoughts, actions and behaviours. Blow this scene up in your mind. Dwell and linger on the images that flow through your mind. Allow your imagination to run free.

Here is my question. What is your intensity number? What number best represents your game face plays?

If your plays are more towards the relaxed side of thinking and behaviour then you may find yourself at around a 4. This is more towards an Ernie Els style of play. If, however, you are more of an upbeat *go get 'em* type of golfer then you will likely choose a number around 6.

To help you put these numbers in perspective, a 2 on our scale probably aligns itself with giving up, while an 8 is so intense that it likely represents being too angry, frustrated or too aggressive in your play.

Your intensity level number is the perfect accompaniment to your game face plays. You now have a series of words and phrases as well as a number that embodies your very best golf. Here are some examples:

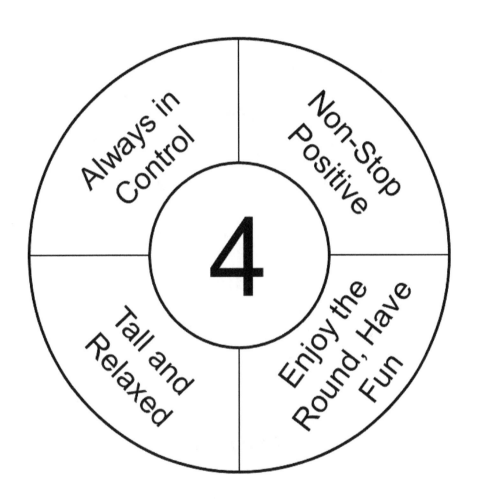

Your Performance Chemicals

If you are curious to know why your game face, and specifically the plays in your game face, are so powerful then let me direct you to a piece of psychological research conducted by Georgia Tech University during the 1994 Soccer World Cup in the U.S.

The final was between Brazil and Italy played on a hot summer's evening at the Rose Bowl in Pasadena, California. The researchers were interested to learn about hormonal change in those who perceive winning and losing. They took testosterone measures from the saliva of Brazilian and Italian fans before the match and again after the match had finished. It was the best player in the world at the time who brought a conclusion to the final - Roberto Baggio, the Italian playmaker, missed his penalty kick to hand Brazil the World Cup. What researchers found was staggering. The average testosterone levels of the Brazilian fans had increased by 28%, while the average levels of the Italians had decreased by 27%.

As Professor Ian Robertson in his brilliant book, *The Winner Effect*, put it: "Events engineered the hormones of hundreds of millions of people in just a few hours."

This is relevant to your golf because how you think, feel, behave and subsequently perform on the course is dominated by the hormones you release. Science has demonstrated that as we start to perceive ourselves playing well, and as we start to believe we can win, our bodies begin to release a powerful combination of performance and feel good chemicals. As success starts to hit you, testosterone and adrenaline - your performance hormones - charge through your bloodstream giving you strength and alertness. You breathe deeper and provide the brain and your muscles with oxygen rich blood. Dopamine and endorphins, your feel good chemicals, give you a profound sense of wellbeing and you will feel less tired and more euphoric.

When you're on the course this blend of performance and feel good hormones supercharges your mindset. You can make better decisions. You find it easier to rip through the ball with complete commitment. Targets appear bigger and you will feel you have more time to get back to the ball. You will feel unbeatable.

In contrast when you feel like you're starting to lose you tend to enter a downward spiral. This losing feeling releases the stress hormone cortisol which, when mixed with the chemical adrenaline that is spreading throughout your body, leads you to feel anxious and fearful. You will experience a nasty sinking feeling and your body seizes up, making coordinated movement tough to deliver.

This is why recording, rehearsing, reinforcing and repeating your game face is important. It's a supercharged process of preparing to play. Remember back to the last chapter, when I introduced you to the scientific belief that the brain and nervous system cannot tell the difference between what is real and what is imagined? It is this principle that underpins rehearsing your game face in your mind, time and time again, as part of your preparation. Reinforce your game face every day and you give yourself a great chance to execute your plays when you step onto the first tee.

Use your game face blueprint daily. It's like charging your cell phone – when running on low you need reminders of greatness.

Carry this with you... always

Champions know their game face. They carry victory with them – always. They hold the image of success in their mind – always. On the course they display their winner's mentality and release a potent mix of adrenaline and testosterone - it's a brew that sees them home under the most intense pressure.

Use your game face before you play as part of a broad package of preparation. To know yourself at your best is a blueprint that *must* be rehearsed daily. Take it to the driving range and don't venture out for a practice round until you are coherent in its verse.

We are going to return to our game face in chapter 7. For now let's unwrap another preparation procedure that will help you play Golf Tough.

5

Plotting Your Course

Kiwi Rod has two rules.

"Rule number one – get the best bag on your shoulder. Rule number two – get out of the golfer's way."

We're standing on the first tee of the Son Vida Golf Club in Mallorca and I'm learning. With the experience of walking the fairways with the world's finest golfers, professional Tour caddies are some of the most informed golf teachers on the planet. A brief glance at your swing and they know where you should aim and where you shouldn't. They have mastered the art of pressure communication - they know what to say, when to say it, and they know when to keep quiet. They are expert sport psychologists!

Kiwi Rod is taking me through some of the important fundamentals of being a Tour caddie – a survivor's guide if you like. His pay has always depended on adhering to his two rules. He admits that getting the best bag is somewhat out of his control - a caddie has to pick up what he can - to survive financially. But his second rule is imperative. Mastering the art of on-course communication takes many years walking the fairways with the differing personalities that grace the premier global tours. Some players like to chat – they are a breed of relaxed casual golfer. For them the banter a caddie can bring to the course is akin to a thought massage for pressure golf. Other golfers demand silence and precise yardages – they don't necessarily want the chat.

But all professional golfers know that an accomplished bag man can save a serious number of shots. They are there to carry the load – literally and metaphorically. They are a sounding board for indecision and a therapist for the angry and upset. A gentle word or a silent nod can ease tension and provide the calming feeling a player needs. The key is to know whether a player appreciates a broken silence when strain is visible.

Back on the first tee, Rod knows my background as a half decent player but is also aware of how little golf I play these days. He points down the right half of the fairway and then to my hybrid. "Just in play Dan – that's all you need." These words are actually soothing, and as a semi-hypnotised golfer I reach for Rod's club of choice. One reasonably hit shot later the ball is sitting up gleefully on the fairway. Kiwi Rod picks up the bag and as we stride off the first tee he starts to tell me about the roads he's travelled.

Kiwi Rod's World

A Tour caddie with over 15 years experience, Rod Gutry (nickname – Kiwi Rod) didn't start his working life walking the world's fairways, but he has always loved giving advice to golfers. As a kid growing up in New Zealand he started to drag a trolley around for mates when they played in local tournaments; helping was always more rewarding than playing for Kiwi Rod. As a talented artist and designer he ended up in sales and marketing for big corporations, but amidst the office commitments his love of golf never abated. Playing to a 9 handicap he could find the sweet spot himself, but he exercised his enjoyment of the game in a different way. Rather than choosing to go on vacation he pitched up on the Australasian Tour from time to time and carried a bag for one of the professionals. He started to learn his trade while basking in the Antipodean sun!

Life changed for Kiwi Rod when, finally bored with the day-to-day drudgery of the office, he resolved to turn a decision to go on a world tour into a career opportunity. He bought himself a ticket to Europe, and rather than restrict his time to soaking up the sights and sounds of Europe's cosmopolitan cities he combined his love of travel with his experiences in golf. He became a professional caddie.

Over the years he has caddied on both the Ladies and the main European Tour, enjoying several tournament victories along the way. And he has used this experience wisely. Settling down with his Spanish wife in Mallorca he started a strategy and course management school at the beautiful Arabella Golf Complex. Both amateur and professional players from all over Europe take time to come and see Kiwi Rod to benefit from his insight into course play. I did the same, and this is what I learnt.

Kiwi Rod's Course Strategies

Know where your risks are and grade them

For Kiwi Rod they are like magnets. And he wants you to meet their negative charge by positively aiming away from them. He bemoans the amount of money he has lost because of the territory beyond the white stakes; the water and the sand have reduced his bank account as well. Rod is well acquainted with the trouble on a golf course, and knows they are number busting nightmares - he wants you to avoid them. And if he was on your bag you'd be exposed to a system that would improve your ability to plot your way around the course helping you to avoid the reload, the wet ball, and the plugged lie.

Kiwi Rod's first strategy is simple - know where your risks are. Tour caddies will, by and large, start their working week at a tournament walking the course for their golfer. They like to get a heads-up on the slopes, the run offs, and the danger zones. When Rod gets to work, observing the course, he makes it his business to befriend the hazards so he can help his player avoid them. He sketches in his own yardage chart and physically colours the obstacles that may prevent him picking up a great cheque for a week's work. With tour courses being fraught with danger his yardage chart tends to be a kaleidoscope of colour!

Rod borrows a process that Jack Nicklaus used to great effect over his career. If it was good enough for the greatest player ever to hold a club, then Rod reckons it might be of value to his paymasters. Nicklaus used to grade the trouble on a golf course, differentiating the most penal from the least punishing obstacles. This strategy helped him make decisions under pressure, and it's a useful one for you to employ to help you play Golf Tough.

I think we'd all agree that the most dangerous part of the course is the section that isn't *on* the course. Find the Out Of Bounds (OOB) with your tee shot and there is only one option – play the shot again with a penalty. If a hole has a stretch of white stakes on one side of the fairway, I suggest your strategy off the tee should be to play away from the side the OOB is on. If, on the other hand, OOB lies both left and right of the fairway play a conservative tee shot.

An OOB encroaching on both sides of the hole should encourage the safe play - a hybrid or long iron ripped down the middle. Short but straight, and out of harm's way.

Kiwi Rod would argue that a slightly less threatening danger than OOB is a water hazard. But lakes, streams, and ponds can be as menacing. Unless the hazard has run dry or you are fortunate enough that your ball has come to rest on the very edge of the hazard there is little to do but drop the ball, again for a penalty shot. Aim away from the water. How you do this may depend on the standard of your golf. For example, a mid to high handicapper can achieve this in simple terms - by aiming and swinging towards a section of the fairway or green furthest from the hazard. A better player, one who has the ball under his control a little more, may prefer to move the ball away from the hazards – left to right or right to left. You are the best judge of what *you* can and can't do with the ball so strategise accordingly.

Out of bounds and water hazards are, by and large, the cruellest trouble spots on the course. These are followed by danger zones such as trees and heavy rough, the order of which will depend on the course (and specifically the holes) you are playing. Once you've eliminated the woodland and the thick stuff your checklist will probably include bunkers, although golfers who play coastal golf may beg to differ about the impact trees have on the game as opposed to sand traps. It is unlikely that those who play a Links course will position trees above bunkers on their list of things to avoid. In contrast, for those of you who tend to play parkland courses, woodlands tend to shadow the fairways you compete on and thus will rank high on your list of things to steer clear of. Naturally, any grading system will be individual to you and to the specific type of course you play regularly.

Finally, at the bottom of your list you may want to consider the inclusion of slopes on and off the fairway. Hitting from a sidehill, downhill, or uphill lie, can always be troublesome and, in my opinion, tougher than striking a ball from light rough. So a grading system will most likely go in this order:

- Out of bounds
- Hazards (yellow and red staked)
- Trees, heavy rough and/or bunkers
- Sloping fairways
- Light rough

Professional golfers aren't always afforded the luxury of playing practice rounds on the course they are competing on. Whilst they may enjoy the benefits of having a caddie walk the course for them to identify the trouble spots, they won't necessarily have had the option to have played on the course themselves. But by the time they tee it up on a Thursday, the first day of a tournament, they usually know the course – its idiosyncrasies, its opportunities, and its challenges pretty well. This is because they will have spent some time studying the course yardage book and will have laid strategic plans appropriately.

Many weekend players will argue that they don't have the chance to prepare to play medals. They are at work during the week or at school. They are too busy with their family life. This simply isn't true - with a bit of commitment there is always time and there are always ways to strategise. Many golfers are a member of a golf club and primarily compete at their home course. They are exposed to the same humps, hollows, and hazards on the same track they will have played week-in week-out (sometimes for many years). This is better preparation than the professionals get themselves. Yet many players spend their weekend medal forging the identical mistakes they've always been guilty of. Is this because you continue to aim straight down the middle irrespective of what hazards may lay ahead of you? Is this because you have never really looked at your course before, in detail, with strategy in mind?

For those of you who like to take yourselves further afield to compete - why not ring ahead and ask the professional shop to send you a yardage planner in the post? In fact many clubs now put a map of their course online. Gathering as much detail as you can will silence the gremlins and quieten your mind on the first tee. It will send a signal of certainty through your body and save you a shot or two per nine.

Knowing the trouble spots before you play helps calm the mind and soothe the nerves when you compete for real.

Get it in play

Kiwi Rod has marked the landscape for you, and your deal in this agreement is to keep the ball away from OOB and water hazards at all costs. Your scores will prosper as a result!

Maybe Kiwi Rod and I are lurching from one obvious statement to the next, yet stroll the course with your average fourball and you'll rarely see a member of the group aim anywhere other than the middle of the fairway or at the flag. And when I say flag, I mean every flag irrespective of its location. Flags cut tight to a pond or a deep bunker are fair game to most golfers, especially to those with less skill - those who have little say on where their ball goes.

Go for a course strategy session with Rod at his home club in Mallorca and he'll knock a couple of shots off your average score by directing you down the safest route towards the hole. If this sounds desperately unexciting then think of the drinks or the few dollars you'll be winning as a result of being a little more cautious!

As Kiwi Rod said to me from the get go: "Put the ball in play". If this means aiming towards the left half of the fairway, because OOB curves in from the right, then aim left. If it means taking a 5 iron off the tee on a 400 yard par 4 because the hole is the tightest you've ever played - then so be it. Give yourself the best chance to remove a triple or double from your scorecard.

The best players work the percentages. They know what they can and can't do, and strive at all times to keep the ball in play.

Take your medicine

Carry Kiwi Rod's voice with you around the course – get the ball in play. This is a great maxim to motivate you to make the right choices out there. It is maybe a philosophy that errs on the side of caution, but it's an attitude that is inherent in Golf Tough, and one that will bring home the bucks more often than not.

If you do hit a shot in the wrong direction – and even the most accurate golfer finds the rough – then Kiwi Rod has the perfect accompaniment to his conservative pre shot plan.

It didn't take long for him to promote his attitude towards bad shots during my course strategy lesson at Arabella. My tee shot on one of the front nine holes finished in a fairway trap some 180 yards away from the green. The lip of the bunker was a little higher than comfortable for the 5 iron shot that I faced. As I stood there, stony faced, wondering what to do, that calm soothing voice interrupted once more. "Take your medicine. Stick to the 70% rule – if you're 70% sure you can pull the shot off go for it. Any less – 69%, 68% - then play safe."

"Take your medicine," is something Kiwi Rod has said a few times over the past decade-and-a-half. Thankfully, it took quite a few holes before he piped up with it, aimed at me – I'd played quite well and stayed trouble free for most of the round until my visit to the teasingly high lipped bunker. By taking one's medicine Rod is emphasising the strategic attitude a golfer should take when a poor shot has left you with a risky decision to make. When half your brain is shouting 'go for it' and the other half is remonstrating with this course of action, the naturally conservative Rod has the 70% rule - a directive that can quieten the devil inside of you. If you're not 70% sure you can pull off the tough shot then take the safe route. If you believe that 7 out of 10 times you'll pull the shot off then go for it.

As a professional golfer I was never the boldest of players, possibly because I was far from an accomplished striker of the ball. But even this level of conservatism sent a wave of confusion through my body. I would usually take the shot on, but Kiwi Rod suggested a slightly safer shot that, if hit properly would clear the lip of the bunker and land some 20 yards short. Although tempted to pull the 5 out I decided to go with

Kiwi Rod's idea and plumped for a 7 iron instead. The added loft gave me that edge of confidence and I swung with a little more freedom than I may have done had I chosen the 5 iron. As a result the shot came out pretty hot and nestled in the short rough just in front of the green. I up and downed for a steady par which gave Rod the opportunity to give me an 'I told you so nod'. I wish I had had Kiwi Rod when I was young golfer to reign in my impulsive youthful mind!

Affect the hole – don't let it affect you

The back stretch of holes on the Son Vida course at the Arabella golf complex is tough. It presents running sloping fairways from tee to green which are encased by trees and bunkers. Like many Mediterranean courses it's an intimidating ride.

But only if you let it be!

The final tip Kiwi Rod gave me was closest to my heart as a sport psychologist. Rod explained that many times over the years he felt that too many players he'd worked with, even the professional ones, allowed the nature of the hole to affect their strategy. Interestingly, he recalled moments on tour when some of the players he worked with would change their strategy (and their swing) according to the length of the hole they had in front of them.

Over the years Rod has observed a pattern that players have a tendency to do particularly well on a certain type of hole and badly on others. For example, he worked with one player whose habit was to hit wayward tee shots on par fives. Kiwi Rod noticed that he tended to get a little too aggressive with his swing, no doubt caused by a focus on trying to birdie the hole. Similarly he worked with a player who rarely made birdies on par 3's and his statistics confirmed an above par stroke average for the shorter holes. Rod felt that he was a little too conservative with his approach play into par 3's – trying to avoid bogeys a little too often, even when the pin was very accessible.

There is often an interaction to be seen between your statistics, course strategy and mindset. Have a look at your averages for the par 3's, 4's and 5's. Are you better at one length than the other distances? If your scores on par 5's are poor it might be because you are trying to force your shots off the tee. The longer holes tend to tease you away from your conservative strategy. It's easy to find yourself seduced into striving for a little extra distance.

Kiwi Rod explained to me that all too often players allow the length of the hole to dictate their mindset. In most rounds he finds himself reminding his players that they shouldn't force a par 5 or ease up on a par 3 or 4. He finds himself repeating the game plan that the players have laid down during the week prior to the tournament. Their job is to *own* their mindset, rather than letting the course dictate their mentality. Make sure *you* are in charge on the course!

Your Strategies

The next time you play a friendly fourball at your home club take Kiwi Rod's voice with you. Allow his ideas to impact your game. Know where the trouble is and do what you can to avoid the hazards. Get the ball in play and take your medicine when you've hit it wide.

Plot your strategies in the build up to your next competitive outing – they'll save you some shots. Golf Tough golfers may not be the best ball strikers or the longest hitters. They may not reach the par 5's in two or carry the ball onto short par 4's but Golf Tough golfers rarely leave shots out there. They get the very most from their ability by playing intelligent, strategic golf. They know that is all they can ask of themselves. That is all they can do.

6

Your Brain's Routine

The first two parts of your Golf Tough preparation are complete. You have some ideas to plot your way around the course intelligently and you have chosen the plays in your game face script.

I want you to learn your game face back-to-front and front-to-back. Write them down and commit them to memory. Put your script by your bedside so you receive a sleepy eyed hit of confidence from its message. Stick a note documenting its details on your fridge - when you're hungry or want to quench your thirst you get to see your game face up close.

You are nearly ready to play Golf Tough. But there are some fine details to cover first – distinction on the course is built from grains of excellence.

You need to develop a process that will help you build confidence *in the moment.* You need a procedure that will help you focus your mind. You need a system that will help clear your thoughts so you can make effective decisions. You need something you can hang onto under pressure. You need a shot routine. And to build a routine to play Golf Tough you need a method that can help you manage the quirks of your brain.

Managing Your PFC

Problem solving, formulating solutions, making decisions, focusing the mind, taking action, and managing emotional impulses are the mental challenges golfers have to tackle before, and after, every shot they play.

It is the front part of our brain, the Pre-Frontal Cortex (or PFC for short) that takes the lead in executing all of these processes. This is the intelligent part of our brain. It is the part that directs and guides us through our day-to-day life. It is the smallest section of the brain but its role in playing golf is vital. It's the part that carries out the course strategies that Kiwi Rod wants you to play. It's the part that enables you to say "This 165 yard shot is a five iron." It's the part that instigates your step into the ball and the movement of the club away from the ball. It is the part that reminds the rest of your brain to relax after you've sliced your tee shot into the trees. It's quite important!

Understanding your PFC is crucial if you want to build a routine that will help you play Golf Tough. If confidence, concentration, control and consistency are your watchwords for success on the course then engaging in PFC-friendly rituals, as you reach the ball, are basic must-haves.

When working with clients I tend to split the routine into three. This kind of progressive structuring promotes a step-by-step set of habits that are easy to digest and straightforward to complete. Let's take each one in turn and build a Golf Tough routine.

Your golf routine should be designed with your Front Brain in mind. It requires you to take control of you!

Preparation – Making Great Decisions

Every great shot begins with a great decision.

Commentators say that the game's psychology lies in its sedentary pace. With plenty of time in-between shots the mind is given the opportunity to wander – too often onto past mistakes and future problems. This is true and it's a challenge that we'll address later in the book. But as a student of the brain I would counter that golf is also psychologically demanding because you are the pilot of the decision making process every step of the way. You are burdened by a decision process on every shot. In contrast, in a sport like tennis, your opponent weighs more heavily on your play. If a shot is struck to your backhand you really only have the decision to play that type of shot. In golf you can choose to play it high, low, left to right and right to left. And in golf the weather elements and surrounding environment impact and impinge on your decision making, more so than for most other sports.

The preparation section of the routine is a time to engage your thinking brain in order to make the crucial decisions the game demands. It starts as we reach the ball, or the tee, and is designed to combat the immediate challenge a golfer faces as he parks his bag or trolley – a flood of information. Where to aim, the location of hazards, the most appropriate target, and weather, are just a few things that the golfer's brain has to filter through. It's easy to get yourself into a mental kerfuffle as you reach the ball with so much going on.

Interestingly, although the PFC is monumentally important in terms of our thinking processes, it's also minute when compared to the rest of the brain. It doesn't have the capacity to hold much information at any one time. And the brain hates to be pulled in loads of directions at once. Doing so prevents us from making great decisions.

With this problem in mind, the preparation part of your routine requires a series of steps that help reduce your brain's workload. I see so many players lean towards their bag and reach for a club without any forethought or analysis of the situation that confronts them. I suggest you take a second to stand behind, or next to the ball, and enjoy a deep breath before you do anything else. Even if you've taken the time to make some calculations as you've walked to the ball I still suggest standing back for the briefest of seconds, just to collect yourself.

One of the simplest ways to structure your decision making process is to ask yourself a question – one that forces an answer. Great questions focus the mind. And on the golf course they are your shortcut to a little thought-out wisdom. So I suggest you quietly ask yourself: "Where do I want to hit my next shot from?"

If nothing else such a question will turn down the volume of less important thoughts intruding on your mind. It clears the PFC and allows it to function optimally. The question will force you to firstly look at the dangers that are up ahead (remember what Kiwi Rod said about dangers!). From this information you get an insight into where you *don't* want to go. You will also build clarity on where you *do* want to go. Conclude the answer to the question by affirming, in your mind, where your *exact* target is. As you will find out, later in this chapter, the brain loves certainty.

You now have a target so it's time to choose a club. To help you do so, here are a couple more questions for you to ask yourself and then for you to answer. "What is the weather doing and what is my lie like?" Then, "What specific shot and specific club will get me to my target?" A gradual collection of detail will avoid a brain overwhelm!

I'm sure an elite player may argue that he or she needs to gather even more information, while a weekend golfer may argue that the whole preparation routine appears long-winded. The truth is everyone's routine will be unique to them. In this chapter I am stressing the importance of developing a routine that adheres to the principles of brain functioning. It is useful to have specific steps in the preparation routine in order to clear the PFC and make an effective decision on club choice and shot selection. How detailed you make it is entirely up to you, but I would strongly recommend the questioning process I have outlined because your brain demands structure and simplicity.

It's not a long process when you break it down and can be completed in less than a minute:

- A breath
- Question: "Where do I want to hit my next shot from?"
- Affirm: "This is my *exact* target."
- Question: "How far is it to my target?"
- Question: "What is the weather doing and what is my lie like?"
- Question: "What specific shot and specific club will get me there?"

There are often complaints of slow play in golf and I don't want to add fuel to a fire that is already burning bright. But two points to note. The presence of a routine may slow things down by a few seconds, but its execution will speed things up – you will hit better shots and spend less time looking in the heavy rough or the trees for your ball. If, however, you are extremely sensitive to the pace of play then start the preparation section of your routine as you are walking to the ball. That's not ideal but I know many people are conscious of keeping play moving. A balance of effective decision making and an eye on keeping play moving is optimal here.

*So many shots are dropped due to poor decisions.
Basic Q&A's help you focus your mind on the task
to make great decisions.*

Performance – A Craving for Certainty

The preparation part of the routine should be left behind and the performance section triggered through a simple cue. Any cue – something you do or something you think – should be specific to the individual. Over the years I've found clients enjoy different types of cues. Some have silently expressed a word in their mind such as "ready" or "commit", while others have employed a physical action such as pulling the club out of the bag, or putting their glove on.

Once triggered, the performance routine is designed to climb the mental mountain that looms large as the golfer prepares to make a swing and hit the ball. That period when you remove your club from your bag is highly psychological because your brain slips into uncertainty mode. "What will happen when I hit this ball?" is the message spreading through your brain (and in many respects shooting through your body). The brain is a prediction-making machine and it loves certainty. In fact it craves certainty. It enjoys thinking ahead, creating an image of the immediate future – a snapshot of how things will pan out. Consider the uncertainty you feel when you walk into a room of strangers at a party or a business networking event. That feeling of 'not knowing' can be enormously uncomfortable. In contrast, think of that feel-good hit of certainty you get when you walk into a room full of friends and family. Every golf shot introduces your brain to the former state - a moment of uncertainty - with the outcome unknown the brain doesn't like this state of being.

In this part of your routine you are required to feed your brain the sweet soothing sound of certainty. To do this I suggest you play around with a combination of cue words, interesting questions, and action led triggers. This is what we'll do now.

Practice Swings

When the performance routine has been triggered I advise clients to start building the *feeling* of certainty through their practice swing. I firmly believe these rehearsal swings can be at the heart of nourishing your brain's readiness to hit the shot. A practice swing is simply a blueprint that you can use and recreate over the ball. To help you get the most from your practice swings, let me pose a question. When you swing at your best what does the motion feel like? Choose a single word to describe your very best swings. Here are a few example answers:

- Committed
- Decisive
- Athletic
- Confident
- Free
- Focused

It is necessary to answer this question to make sure the word you choose is one you can action. This is because I want you to act out the word as you take your practice swings. Let me explain.

Once you've taken the club out of the bag I want you to take some practice swings in the style of your chosen word. If your word is "committed" I want you to take some *committed* swings. I want you to move the club away from the ball with one goal in your mind – to feel *committed* throughout your swing. I want you to reach the top of your swing feeling *committed* and I want you to swing down and through the hitting area in a *committed* way. I want you to complete your follow-through with full *commitment*. If your chosen word is "focused" I want you to take your practice swing with the strict intention of *feeling* focused and *being* focused.

Take charge of this process. Immerse your brain in certainty. "I am swinging freely. That feels great. I'm going to recreate this feeling of freedom over the ball. I am going to swing freely when hitting the shot for real." Creating your physical blueprint, while forcing that sense of certainty to the surface, plunges you into a deep feeling of focus and increases your chances of a successful shot.

And we can go even further. Take your practice swings with your keyword in mind, and as you swing through the hitting area, *feel* the shot you want to make. Explore your kinaesthetic sense fully. Allow the feeling of an incredible strike rip through your hands and arms and up through your torso. As you swing through, in your mind's eye see the shot rifle away on a pin perfect trajectory. Give the visual stores in your brain a gift – let them experience a perfect ball flight.

With certainty vibrating through your mind I want you to unleash even more confidence into your nervous system by asking yourself a positive question, "What does an incredible shot look like?" Answer the question with a picture-perfect inner movie that brings to life the ripped shot you want to produce. A reminder of your best shot for the given situation should carry with it a wave of unstoppable momentum!

The Walk and the Set Up

You're nearly ready to play the shot. But first it's wise to maintain the impetus of certainty you've built. Let me do that by asking you what a confident walk into the ball looks, and feels, like. Some say 'tall'. Some say 'big steps'. Others simply say 'confident – it looks and feels confident'. The point being, I want you to walk into the ball in this manner. This not only helps you to continue to stay focused, it also helps you increase your certainty.

I'm unsure if you've ever experienced a negative feeling, when you stand over the ball, but a lot of my clients have. You may recognise it. I'm referring to the times when your setup feels uncomfortable – when it lacks solidity. Throughout my golfing career I've always had times when my setup felt sloppy, and the people I've worked with over the years have reported the same. With this aberration in mind I'd like you to choose a word that represents the feeling you get when you feel great over the ball. Here are some examples:

- Athletic
- Solid
- Tall
- Ready
- Stable
- Comfortable
- Compact
- Balanced

Once you've walked to the ball with confidence, I want you to get into a setup that feels great to you. So if you choose "balanced" I want you to walk confidently into a balanced setup. If you choose "solid", I want you to walk confidently into a solid setup.

Wait or Go

Once you've climbed into your stance, once you've setup to the ball, then it's useful to have a consistent pattern to the physical part of your routine. Are you a golfer who likes to settle and look at the target a few times before you move the club away from the ball? Or are you a golfer who likes to hit 'em quick?

My advice is to make your mind up whether you are a wait or a go golfer. A wait golfer takes a minimum of two looks at the target and a waggle or two. A go golfer will take a solitary glance and then pull the trigger.

Whether you wait or you go, your objective as you stand over the ball is simple – recreate the blueprint you formed during your practice swing. Do so with conviction and confidence. Most of all - do so with certainty!

Swing with your cue word in mind – swing with commitment or swing in a decisive manner. Remember, the key is to let your mind be absorbed in the process of delivering your club into the ball with complete certainty.

But I like to Blank MY Mind....

Many golfers tell me they like to blank their mind when they swing. They prefer to think of nothing. They don't like a swing thought, and they may repel the idea of swinging in the style of a keyword.

That's fine. Whatever works for you, works for you. But I'm unsure you can play consistent golf if you simply 'blank your mind'. As we shall discuss in the next section the brain is constantly firing. It loves something to grab hold of – something it can place its attention on. This isn't the same as over-thinking. I'm not suggesting the route to a clear mind is to have three or four swing thoughts as you swing back and through. I'm not suggesting that you try to control every moving part of your swing. I'm not suggesting that you strive to consciously turn your shoulders, swing your arms up, cock your wrists, maintain your spine angle, release the clubhead through impact, and shift your weight into the follow through. This isn't what I'm saying at all. I'm suggesting you swing in the style that encompasses your best. It really is that simple.

And for those who want to preach that the so called 'Zone' is a product of a silent mind, I say this. The 'Zone' is *not* 'no thinking'. The 'Zone' is *not* 'no thought'. The 'Zone' is *less* thought. And paradoxically, by trying to blank your mind you invite thought in. The act of suppressing thought promotes thought.

I believe that golfers need a series of steps, verbal and physical cues, and triggers, that not only build a momentum of certainty, but also help the brain pinpoint its focus and make it easier to keep a clear mind. The 'Zone' can't be forced. You give yourself the best opportunity to step into that sweet spot of high performance if you have calculated steps to follow in your routine that occupy your attention on the right things, and which build certainty and confidence. A clear mind, not a blank mind, is a better way to view the 'Zone'.

So feel free to add a swing thought into the mix. Just don't have too many thoughts over the ball. Over-thinking kills coordination and renders you Golf Tight rather than Golf Tough.

Here's a summary of your new performance routine:

- Club pulled out of the bag triggers the performance routine
- Practice swings in the style of your keyword
- Question: "What does an incredible shot look like?"
- A confident walk to the ball
- Your best feeling setup
- Swing in the style of your key word (with a swing thought if you choose)

I'd like to emphasise, this is a suggested routine. Give these steps a go. If it feels too long for you then build a routine on your own terms. All I ask is that you keep, at the forefront of your mind, the notion that the brain likes to drag you down into a feeling of uncertainty. It is your job to combat this destructive feeling and, if you want to consistently play Golf Tough, you need to find way to push through into certainty mode.

Post Shot - Using your Energy

The ball has gone.

It's when the ball soars into the distance that golf provides an injection of energy. And you have to do something with it!

Your post shot routine begins when the shot ends. Almost as soon as you experience the sensation of the clubhead colliding with the ball you get to see the fruits of your labour. Very rarely do you have to wait that long to see where the ball has finished – its initial ball flight gives you the instant clues you need to know whether you've hit a good shot or not.

Wherever your shot flies more often than not you will experience a surge of energy. Miss your target by a distance and you'll likely feel a rush of frustration. Or you may let anger engulf you. Alternatively, you may crash and feel despondent. In contrast, find the sweet spot and you'll fire a positive emotion through your nervous system.

You need to do something with this energy - allow extreme emotions to take over and your PFC will soon close off. Those cool, calm effective decisions will quickly climb out the window and your ability to help your brain deal with uncertainty will diminish. No chance of Golf Tough. The likelihood of a great score will fade away.

The 3 C Check-In

I'm unsure whether you can control the first thought you have after you've hit a shot and I find it important to give golfers some breathing space. If you've hit a terrible shot by all means allow your brain and body to express its response. Don't suppress the nervous system's natural inclination to react. Everyone is a little different with their coping mechanisms and everyone should be allowed to follow their preferred path.

I do however believe you can *choose* to manage your second, third and fourth thoughts. And with this in mind I introduce golfers to a '3 C check-in' process.

- Calm down
- Climb up
- Clear to go

If you find the red mist starting to descend – your heart rate increasing and a tightening of your body (accompanied by some expletives) – then it's time to calm down. Alternatively, if you find yourself getting despondent – when all feels lost and helpless, and you're ready to throw in the towel – then it's time to climb up. As part of your 'check in' procedure feel free to give yourself the all clear. Many shots you'll hit will be simply ok – neither exciting nor demoralising. If you hit one of these 'check in' as 'clear to go', put your club back in the bag and move on.

The handy thing about the 'check in' process is that you can use your game face script to calm yourself down or climb yourself up. Allow me to give you a couple examples.

A game face of 'Tall and Confident' can help you climb up if you need to. Standing tall and enjoying the freedom you have to experience walking with confidence is the perfect tonic when despondency starts to kick in.

A game face of 'Relax and Slow' assists in calming you down. Reminding yourself to relax and purposefully slowing down your walking pace counters the rush of adrenaline you feel when anger attacks your body and eats away at your mind.

Ultimately this process comes down to you staying in control of yourself. We will go into more detail about how you can achieve this in the next section of Golf Tough.

Your Brain's Routine

The inclusion of the word brain in the title of this chapter is for a reason. Your routine is not your pre-shot routine nor is it your basic shot routine. It is your brain routine. Why? Because every thought you have, every thought you experience, gears towards success or failure.

The routine is a routine for your PFC. It's a set of habits for your front brain. It's a repeatable note stuck to your intelligent brain so you can make the most effective decisions under pressure, so you can raise your certainty at will, and so you can cope with the immediacy of failure that golf so cruelly delivers.

The brain routine is the perfect accompaniment to the practice ideas we laid out in the last section of the book. Uniting Golf Tough practice and preparation protocols enables you to train body and mind. The psych drives the physical and the physical drives the psych. I want you to steer both. That is what champions do.

7

Preparing to Win

Many fans, watching professional sport from the outside, misunderstand the notion of a winning mentality. In my experience a competitor needs to have a *will to win* as he or she competes. But the motivation to win whilst competing is only a *part* of the definition of a winning mindset. Ask the world's leading sports coaches and they will tell you that a winning mindset is also one that is fully *prepared* to compete.

Winning doesn't *just* happen on the day of your sporting war. Winning happens *before* a competitor steps onto the first tee. Winning means being ready – physically, emotionally, intellectually and mentally. Winning means knowing exactly what you have to do to give yourself the greatest possible chance to compete at your very best.

Those golfers who expend energy on being thoroughly prepared – knowing their game face, their course strategies, and their brain's routine – will give themselves the very best chance of playing to their max. They have set up an opportunity to win!

The link between a winning mentality and the art of being prepared is probably not a major announcement. You may be well versed in this connection already. But what *is* perhaps less obvious about a winning mindset is that those who are prolific in their win ratio are brilliant at *ignoring* the 'idea of winning' as they compete. That sounds strange right? Let me explain by detailing the mindsets of some high profile winners.

Winning Mentalities

When double Olympic and World Championship Gold medallist Mo Farah steps onto the track to compete in the 5,000 or 10,000 metres he is there to win. He wants to win as much as anyone else. But like all great champions when his race is underway he parks all thoughts of winning and settles his mind onto the things he has to *do* to win. For Mo these things will include getting the correct pace, and finding the right positioning in the field as the race progresses. Mo Farah wants to win but whilst competing he is focused on the *process* of winning.

Likewise, when the greatest Olympian of all time, Michael Phelps, enters the swimming pool arena he has an insatiable desire to win. He wants to pulverise the opposition. But he knows he has to put winning aside for the duration of the race. He knows he will give himself the best chance of winning if he wraps his mind tightly within the confines of the thoughts he has to think about, and the actions he has to execute to find his personal excellence. He knows if he does this then he has done all he can to touch the wall in first place.

When Rafa Nadal and Novak Djokovich and Roger Federer step onto the court - they want to win. They want to beat the player at the other end of the court. They want to win badly. That is why they have trained every day for many years. That is why they have sweated bucket loads in pursuit of excellence. That is why they have served and volleyed and hit forehands and backhands time and time again until their hands have blistered. But when they stand on the baseline in the first game to serve or to receive, their minds are pinpointed towards executing their plays shot by shot, game by game, and set by set. They shift their attention away from winning and they allow their focus to rest on competing with unrelenting confidence and unyielding focus. They concentrate on the strategies they have set themselves in the lead up to the game – the ones that will give them the best chance of beating the opposition in front of them, and they resolve to stick to these strategies under the most intense pressure.

Champions in sport are champions because they exercise the right mindset as they compete. They yearn for victory but they know that when they take to the court, or the course, or the pitch, they have to put their mind in a different place. Winning is always there, but the end game shrinks away from the spotlight and rests in the back of their mind. They cast their focus firmly on the *process* of performance.

*Champions compete intelligently as much as they
do passionately. This means they put winning
aside as they compete.*

Process versus Outcome

Perhaps, to the sports observer, it looks as if the one who 'wants it the
most' is the one most likely to get it – the win that is. It's a romantic
ideal that will follow sport forever. And indeed there is some truth to
this. The more someone wants something the more effort they will put
in. But unfortunately effort isn't 100% correlated to outcome. The view
that a 'win at all costs' mentality is the be-all-and-end-all in sports isn't
completely true. Let's use our examples from above to explain this
concept further.

If an athlete like Mo Farah spends the entire race focused on winning
he may release too much adrenaline through his nervous system and get
too excited. As a consequence he may start his race too fast. He has to
keep his urge to win in check otherwise he'll go off at too quick a pace
– one he'd be unable to maintain. Similarly he has to keep his desire to
win at the back of his mind as he enters the home straight. An athlete
who gets overly excited as the race comes to an end is one who will
tighten up. The more your body tightens the less you will be able to
perform. For Mo Farah to kick for home in the last 200 metres he needs
to stay relaxed because speed is governed by a body that is loose and
supple. Interestingly Mo Farah's winning mentality comprises of
focusing on his running tasks rather than winning itself.

A swim race is similar to competitive athletics. If Michael Phelps spent
the entire race concerned with winning he'd give himself more chance
of finishing in a silver or bronze position (rather than the gold he has
become accustomed to!). If a swimmer who is obsessed with winning
finds himself losing after a couple of lengths it's unlikely he'll remain
calm, patient, and focused. He'll probably panic and he'll lose his
composure. He'll trigger a stress response and he'll sky rocket his
anxiety levels. In contrast, the champion swimmer trusts his stroke. If
he is lagging behind the leaders he reminds himself of what he has to
do to get back into the race. He knows that remaining relaxed is the
perfect energiser in the given situation. A winning mentality is prepared
and poised!

Sporting champions want to win. That truth is what, in part, helps them to hold the trophy aloft or cash the big cheque. But when they stand on the start line, or in our case on the first tee, they are brilliant at putting winning aside. They focus their minds tightly on the things they have to do to win. They are primarily concerned with the process of performance. This 'process' is something I call a script, and we have already started to write yours.

The outcome is driven by the process. Focus relentlessly on the process for the best possible outcome.

Your Performance Script

The performance script is simple and revolves around the contents of the previous three chapters. The script looks like this:

- Game face
- Course strategies
- Brain routine

Your game face, your course strategies, and your brain's routine are important components of your golf because they are the cogs you can look to control out on the course. They incorporate a series of thoughts, actions, and behaviours that you can align yourself with as you compete under pressure. *Think* and *do* your game face as you compete. *Think* and *do* your course strategies as you compete. *Think* and *do* your brain's routine as you compete. Carry them with you from the moment you climb out of your car in the golf club's car park to the time you tee off, and throughout the whole round – front nine and back nine.

When you go play I want you to execute your performance script. I want you to stick with it religiously. I want you to stick to your game face like glue. I want you to execute the course strategies you've committed to. And I want you to nail your brain's routine every time.

Keep thinking and doing them if you are playing well. Be relentless with them – make them your golfing bible. They are useful guides to come back to when you are playing poorly – refer to them if you hit a few poor shots or have a couple of lousy holes.

- *Hit it out of bounds – get back to your script*
- *Miss a short putt – get back to your script*
- *Shank it in the water – get back to your script*
- *Playing against strong opposition – get back to your script*
- *A tight intimidating hole up ahead – get back to your script*

If you do this you will give yourself the best chance of having the best possible outcome you can have. I can't guarantee what that will be. I can't say that every time you execute the three components in your script that you'll shoot under your handicap or pick up the money. Results cannot be forced, but they *can* be massaged.

The next section (the Performance Section) of Golf Tough will give you practical ways to execute your performance script optimally. With the right mindset techniques - you can get more from your game face, your strategies, and your brain's routine. But there are still things you can do prior to playing to ensure you have a fully loaded script and that you are prepared to go play Golf Tough.

Rehearsing your Script

Sport psychologist William Straub, from Ithaca College New York, demonstrated the extraordinary power of the mind and its role in improving performance. In a revolutionary test he asked students to throw 50 darts at a board and then embark on a special training program. After initial scores were counted he split the students up into different groups. Some were told not to play darts again until they came back for another test eight weeks later. Another group practiced throwing darts for 30 minutes, five days a week, for eight weeks. A third group alternated between physical practice and picturing themselves throwing darts. They were told to see themselves positioned at the throwing line, to feel the dart in their fingers, to feel it release, to see and hear the dart hitting the bull's eye, and to allow themselves to experience the satisfaction they would feel at throwing accurate darts.

After eight weeks, the group that hadn't practiced physically or mentally showed no improvements. The group that practiced daily improved by an average of 67 points. But the group that used practice combined with 'picturing throwing' improved by up to 165 points: an incredible improvement and a remarkable difference between the mentally trained group and the group who just trained physically.

By asking people to 'mentally rehearse' Straub demonstrated that sports skills can be developed more quickly and executed better when training covers both body and mind. His scientific findings, alongside outcomes from other similar research studies, demonstrate the benefits of training mindset and mentality. This is what I'd like *you* to do.

The 1% Rule

Do you know how long 1% of your day is? I'm sure all you mathematics whizzes are there already. 1% of your day is *about* 15 minutes.

I'd like you to commit to mentally rehearsing your performance script for 1% of your day. This means taking a little time to picture your game face, your course strategies, and your brain's routine.

The best way to do this is to utilise short pockets of time to run through your script. For example, you may have five minutes on the train heading into work to imagine yourself on the course brilliantly executing the plays in your game face. Similarly, you may think about your course management strategies as you prepare your evening meal.

There are plenty of occasions during a day when, engaged in mundane activities, you can mentally rehearse your script. When you eat, when you wash, or when you're chilling on the sofa – all these are perfect moments to enjoy thinking about your script. These are great times to choose to dwell on success.

"In the medal this Saturday I am going to keep to my script religiously. I am going to execute my game plays relentlessly. What does that look like? What does that feel like? I am going to stick to my strategies – I know how important they are. I am going to execute my brain's routine with perfection. What does my preparation routine look like? What does my performance routine feel like? What am I going to do every time post shot?"

Sporting champions are known for their ability to exercise their imagination. I want you to do so yourself. This is your opportunity to spend a few moments acting like one of the world's best players.

If a play in your script is to stay 'Tall and Committed' I want you to imagine yourself doing this on a daily basis. Envision playing golf in a 'Tall and Committed' way. Allow your inner movie to settle on complete commitment on the golf course. Let it rest on standing tall no matter what. You hit a lousy shot - you're tall. You dunch it out of the bunker – you're tall. In your mind be ruthless with 'Tall and Committed'. Swing in a committed way. Walk with a 'Tall and Committed' swagger. Stroke your putts with commitment. As you *watch* yourself play 'Tall and Committed' allow a sense of commitment to wash over you. Sit yourself up in your chair and drive your own physiology. I want you to experience a remorseless, merciless, and unremitting sense of commitment.

The days before you tee it up are the times I'd like you to be very clear in your mind – you are going to play golf in the style of your script. The weather won't move you from your script. Nor will the opposition. Nor will the state of the course. You are going to swing with your script in mind. You are going to stroke your putts while executing your script. You are going to move from shot to shot walking in the style your script's game face details. You are going to explode out of the sand to two feet because you have stuck to your brain's routine.

This process isn't a flowery touchy feely task. I don't want you to engage in exercises that are nothing short of exploring high performance. This is a task that engages the mind and allows your body to experience the feeling of inner excellence. This feeling is crucial because it is your release for outer accomplishment. Your 1% time is your blueprint for toughness. It opens a catalogue of pictures that nourishes your mind with excellence.

Golf Tough is about being relentless on the course. It is a relentless focus, a relentless set of behaviours, a relentless way of thinking, all of which feed towards a relentless way of feeling. By going through this process you are evoking the feelings of a champion. You are warming a superior mindset. You are enjoying that inner feeling of distinction.

Create your winning blueprint before you play.
Rehearse it relentlessly. Then go do it!

That Winning Mindset

"I want to win. I want to win this club knockout really badly. To give myself the best opportunity of winning I am going to stick to my script. I am going to go through my brain's routine on every shot no matter what. I am going to act out my game face plays from the first hole to the last hole. I am going to play intelligent golf and stick with my course strategies no matter how my score progresses.

If I start to think about winning on the course I'm going to gently remind myself to re-focus on my script. I know that if I get my script right I will play with focus, certainty and control. I know if I get my script right I will give myself the best chance to take my practice ground game onto the course. I know if I get my script right I give myself a great chance to perform under pressure. If I get my script right I know I will give myself the opportunity to play at my best and win the club knockout."

And Onto Golf Tough...

Champions win in their mind first. Then they go play Golf Tough. A winning mindset is a product of the steps you commit to long before you grace the first tee. Your first shot isn't the first shot at all. Your first putt isn't the first stroke you will have taken on the greens. Your mind and body, readying for a game of Golf Tough, will have rehearsed those moments time and time again.

Your Golf Tough credit is financed through a preparation procedure that draws on your personal highlights reel, your strategic nous, and the confidence techniques you have enveloped in a brain-based routine. These three indispensable processes are available to golfers who compete at the top, or for those lower down the golf chain: the ones who enjoy the battle of the monthly medal or the club knockout competition. It's available even for those who just enjoy smelling the flowers along the way. Golf Tough means better shots, and better shots builds better scores, and better scores make the flowers smell sweeter!

In the next section, after a quick summary of the previous few chapters, we're going to explore ways to supercharge your script. You're going to take complete control on the golf course. You're ready to play Golf Tough, so let's go do it.

Section 2 Summary

Driving Your Golf Tough Preparation

Chapter Four

1. Know you at your best - memory holds clues to high performance.
2. Record the plays in your game face – they are chemically underpinned.
3. Combine your game plays with your intensity sweetspot.

Chapter Five

1. Have a set of course strategies ready so you can play intelligent golf.
2. Know where your risks are and keep it in play.
3. Take your medicine… always!

Chapter Six

1. Develop a brain based routine to manage your PFC.
2. There are 3 parts to your routine – preparation, performance, and post shot.
3. The Zone is 'less' thought, not 'no' thought.

Chapter Seven

1. A winning mentality includes preparation.
2. Winning mindsets tend to ignore winning while they compete.
3. Rehearse your script – daily!

8

Your First Controller

You are in charge. You are the director. You get to dictate. You are in control.

When I say this I'm not talking about the golf swing. I don't think anyone can ever have complete control of their swing. I don't think anyone ever will. It's too complex a motion. It is outside our human capabilities to determine an exact movement at any given time. A sound repetitive golf swing is important, but 100% consistency is a fairy-tale proposal.

I'm not talking about the ball either. The flight and positioning of that little white Titleist or Nike is subject to the subtle nuances of the course and the unsubtle hits of weather that can bombard fairway and green. A bounce here, a change of condition there – an environment that is out of your control is what confronts you on the first tee.

The swing and the ball are out of our complete control. And yet we let these factors wind us up the most. A tight swing, and a lost ball - a poorly struck shot and a bad bounce. These are the things that get us mad on the course, yet we know, before we play any round, that we cannot guarantee perfect swings or to hit 100% of the fairways and greens in regulation.

So, let me be clear - when I speak of control on the golf course I am talking about being in charge of something you *can* actually control. What precisely is that? The fact is - all you can control on the course is your *performance script*.

To give yourself the best chance of playing Golf Tough you have prepared thoroughly. You have taken time to think about, and come up with, the plays in your game face. You have plotted the course and you now have appropriate course strategies. You have also designed a routine that will help your brain to focus and your body to swing with certainty and confidence.

Your game face, your course strategies, and your brain's routine, are in your golf bag and ready to go. These are the three things I want you to get right on the course. There can be no room for compromise – make every shot count. I want 89 not 90. I want 79 not 80. I want 69 not 70. This means you must tune into perfecting the plays in your game face. It requires the will to carry out your course strategies with pinpoint precision. And it entails a disciplined mind, attuned to every action, every motion and every thought that goes into your brain's routine. No one can ever play perfect golf, but *everyone* can execute a *perfect* performance script.

Golf Tough doesn't include an in-between. You are either in or you are out. As you will learn in this section of the book, Golf Tough can be compromised by the nature of your brain. We will work on ways to stay sensitive to your script and return to it if you get distracted. But, from the outset, strive to be stubborn with your Golf Tough approach. From the moment you step onto the practice ground or into the golf net to hit some warm up shots, your mind must be attuned to your performance script.

So now you need to know how you can take a firm hold of your performance script. Remember my message to you in the last chapter - *think* and *do* your game face as you compete. *Think* and *do* your course strategies as you compete. *Think* and *do* your brain's routine as you compete. This is your objective on the golf course. This takes care of playing Golf Tough and ultimately slots you into a mindset and a competitive mentality that helps you shoot the very best score you possibly can. This section of the book will give you the tools to *think* and *do*! It's been written to help you start to take control of you, irrespective of the challenge you face as your round commences.

You Controlling You

I'm not much of a gamer but I can see the attraction. Step into the world of Tiger Woods, or a U.S. Marine, or an all action hero ready to take on an alien nation invading earth, and let your imagination run wild - live a life less ordinary! Some of the mental side of golf is related to using your imagination, and I see the fun in exercising this mental muscle whilst getting lost in another world. The ability to take control of a sporting icon, a super human, or a figure from a planet far, far away can be liberating and invigorating.

And the emphasis must be on the word *control*. Gaming is about taking *control* of someone else or something else and guiding that character through the trials and challenges that are thrown at them. To reach the end unscathed or to win the trophy, your control has to be precise – a wrong direction, an unsure move, or a mistimed motion can send you back to the beginning or can hand the tournament to another victor.

Control in the world of gaming has changed over the years. For me, as a teenager, it used to be directed by a joystick. Today it's by something called a controller. It's no longer a clumsy 'stick' with an over-sized button. It's sleek. It's designed for speed. It's designed for dexterity. It's designed for hand, fingers, and brain to work in harmony for real time control.

Your golf mindset controllers are similar. They are built for speed. They can be applied in the moment. They are built for dexterity. They can be used in any golfing environment, on any course, in any country. They have followed you your whole life and you use them consciously and subconsciously every minute of every day. You carry them with you, always.

You have two controllers that you can use to execute and manage your performance script – your body language and your self-talk. These are the two directors you can use to help you play Golf Tough. You can use them to win!

And if it's raw speed you are after – if an instant surge of adrenaline is required, or perhaps a subtle shift down towards relaxation is needed, there is an American psychology researcher who is showing the world how to use one of your controllers to optimise your performance.

Your outcome, your score, is dictated by your
ability to control yourself as you move
from hole to hole.

The Story of Amy Cuddy

I'm unsure if Associate Professor Amy Cuddy enjoys a round of golf but I *am* sure she'd enjoy the impact her research can have on the game. She works at Harvard University and she is pioneering studies into nonverbal behaviour, hormonal change, and performance.

The premise of her work over the last few years has been simple. She has tried to bring scientific credibility to the old and worn idea that body language makes a difference to how we feel and subsequently impacts upon how we perform. Her story is inspiring and heart-warming and explains the motive behind her interest in the link between body language and performance.

Cuddy had been an intelligent and gifted student bound for a first class career in whatever profession tickled her intellectual fancy. But a terrible car crash at 19 years of age nearly put an end to her vocational ambitions. During the incident she was thrown from the car and woke up in a head injury rehabilitation ward. She was told her IQ had dropped considerably. She was withdrawn from college and informed that a university degree was unobtainable.

However, she refused to accept what others felt was fact. She decided to carry on at university and continued to work at her degree. Although it took her four years longer than her peers, her hard work (and bravery) paid off and she eventually graduated. Following her degree success she was accepted into Princeton as a postgraduate. But when she arrived at one of the world's leading academic institutions she felt an imposter. She had to deliver talks and she had to participate in groups with exceptionally bright young people. She felt she was inferior, unable to work alongside extraordinary minds.

It was only when her mentor, Professor Susan Fiske, persuaded her to keep going that she decided to stay and stick with it. Professor Fiske suggested something simple - an elegant solution for her complex thoughts and feelings. She told Cuddy to 'fake it'. She suggested that she should simply act with confidence at all times. She should act like she belonged at Princeton with all the other clever students. She told her to do every talk she was asked to do, but to do so in the most confident way she could. She told her to keep doing the presenting, the talks, and the group activities, no matter how terrified she was and no matter how lacking in confidence she was.

And so she did these things. And she kept doing them. Over five years she presented and presented and talked and talked. She did these activities with as much confidence as she could muster. And, over the course of the five years she spent at Princeton, she very slowly started to become exactly what she was striving to pretend to be at the beginning of her programme – a confident, self-assured student. She had become what she had faked.

Power Posing

Amy Cuddy is now an Associate Professor at Harvard University. Her life experience has led to a fascination with nonverbal behaviour, emotion, and power. Specifically, her research has targeted the effects body language has on hormonal change and subsequent performance effects. Her findings are dramatic, illuminating, and should have an impact on all our lives.

In her research Cuddy placed participants in a number of poses she labelled as 'power poses'. To give you an idea of what they looked like, one was called 'The Superman' (picture Superman having just landed near a disaster situation, hands on hips, standing as tall as possible, chest pushed out - I think you get the picture!). Essentially she was asking people to fake dominance and to fake power.

Cuddy asked participants to hold these power poses for a couple of minutes and then she measured any hormonal changes that might have taken place over this short period. She discovered that by simply placing people into these powerful positions participants had an increase in testosterone levels and a decrease in the stress hormone, cortisol. Notably, the power poses also increased the participants' appetite for taking risk. Cuddy demonstrated that our bodies can change how we think and how we feel through hormonal change. Our bodies can change our mind.

Cuddy furthered her research by showing that a change of body language and subsequent hormonal shifts can make a difference to performance. She had suspected that it was in evaluative situations where a difference would be seen most graphically. So she set about testing her theory and indeed found that those who went through a process of power poses before a job interview were more successful during the interview process than those who were asked to portray low status poses before an interview. She claimed that the difference between the two groups (low status and power pose) was that the power pose interviewees showed greater presence. They spoke passionately and confidently and they were more captivating and looked more comfortable.

What Cuddy has done through her use of scientific research is to demonstrate that using your body language can alter outcomes. She is careful to explain that whilst her project might have started out as a 'fake it to make it' study, results made it clear that the term 'fake' wasn't accurate. Cuddy now describes the intentional use of body language as 'be it to become it'.

In short, act powerfully, think powerfully and develop the potential to perform powerfully.

Mind follows body as much as body follows mind. To relax or to energise are states of body as much as states of mind.

The Mind Body Link

Let me be clear. I don't think walking around like superman is going to help you reduce your handicap by five shots! It's not going to help the scratch golfer win the US Open or British Open. Alone, it won't promote the promising golfer to PGA Tour status.

But, taking control of how you hold yourself, how you walk and how you project yourself helps you take control of your performance script. I call this mind body link your *body controller*. It enables you to turn up the volume of your game face plays. It helps you emphasise certainty and focus as you walk through your brain's routine. And it helps you commit to the course strategies you have laid out in the run up to your competition.

Your body controller emphasises an important two way process – where mind meets body and body meets mind. As much as your psychology affects the functioning of your body, so how you hold your body also affects your brain. This is something scientists call a *positive feedback loop*.

I want all my clients to take ownership of the loop between their mind and body. I want all my clients to use their body controller for every shot and between every shot. And this is the process I want *you* to utilise. I want you to use your body controller to find Golf Tough. I want you to use your body controller between putting green and first tee to inject yourself with a dash of confidence. I want you to stand tall on the first tee. I want you to walk to the ball holding yourself like Woods, like Mickelson, like Nicklaus. Never ever compromise with your body controller – have it switched on at all times.

On the golf course your body controller consists of four functions or buttons:

- How you hold yourself
- How you walk
- Your actions
- Your breathing pattern

You can choose to use these functions or press these buttons at any time, no matter the state of play, no matter the weather, no matter the course, no matter who you are playing and no matter the tournament you are competing in. If you make a bogey you can choose to hold yourself in a manner that befits confidence. If you miss a short putt you can choose to take some deep breaths. If a relaxed performance is your preferred mode of play you can choose to walk slowly between shots and holes.

If you want to swing with commitment you can choose to rip through the ball in a committed way. I want you to use these buttons on your body controller to take charge of your performance script. That is all you need to do to play Golf Tough and give yourself the very best chance to shoot a low score. And it starts with your controllers.

When, and how often, you use your body controller is determined by you. But you must take charge – you are responsible.

Controlling your Performance Script

The Plays in your Game Face

Take a little time to reflect on the plays in your game face. We're going to use your body controller to work them. To illustrate how this is done let's use an example. John, my client, has four plays in his game face:

- Tall and confident
- Commit at all times
- Walk slow and be patient
- Belief on the greens

If I was to accompany John onto the course I'd be asking him to use his body controller to ensure he carried out his plays. I'd ask John to stand tall and express confidence as often as possible. I'd want his body to project certainty. I'd want his body to exude confidence, even if he wasn't feeling it. This isn't fake. This is a decision. This is a way of being. As Amy Cuddy says, it's not about faking it, it's about becoming it. Using his body controller to stay 'tall and confident' before every shot and after every shot, before every hole and after every hole, is what I'd demand from John.

I'd like John to *act* with commitment as often as he felt it necessary. If he experienced a sensation akin to fear then I'd ask him to walk with commitment and hold himself with commitment. What do you think John might look like? It's hard to articulate on paper but I'm sure you could demonstrate a committed walk or a committed posture if I asked you to. I'd also want John to swing with commitment, but we'll cover this in a little more detail later.

John could also use his body controller to walk slow and stay patient. To walk slow he'd press his 'walk' button and to stay patient he could use the breathing function on his control panel. If he's made a triple bogey down the fifth, after a solid start, taking a few deep breaths could calm his nervous system and relax his tensing body. Breathing lifts the red mist as it descends and clears the mind from the unwanted clutter and the mental baggage that comes with frustration.

Similarly, I'd like John to walk onto the greens with complete belief. To do this he might choose to incorporate being 'tall and confident'. Or perhaps he might strive to hold himself in a relaxed manner. Maybe the sensation of belief for John is more towards a nonchalant state of mind, rather than portraying an aggressive and upbeat demeanour.

Remember, your game face is most meaningful to you, and you will have to use your body controller to evoke the personal feelings that underpin *your* plays. They are yours and no one else's.

Your Brain's Routine

Your body controller is particularly useful in delivering impactful brain routines. You can use your body language – how you hold yourself, how you walk, your actions and your breathing pattern – to build confidence and pinpoint focus and subsequently hit consistent shots.

How you use your body controller in your routine is dependent on the steps you have put in place. You can use your body controller to:

- Take a deep breath to start your preparation routine (breathing pattern)

- Stand upright and act decisively as you go through your decision making process (how you hold yourself)

- Withdraw the club from your bag in a committed manner (your actions)

- Take free swings (your actions)

- Walk to the ball with confidence (how you walk)

- Get set up in an athletic position (how you hold yourself)

- Swing smoothly (your actions)

- Hold your finish no matter where it goes (how you hold yourself)

This is such a simple system to execute. Strive to keep fantastic body language throughout your routine no matter what. Use the different functions or buttons as you work through your routine to fuel your focus and confidence and to keep your brain happy. When you use your body controller to manage your game face, your strategies, and your brain's routine you'll put yourself in a mindset to swing at your best.

A Golf Tough golfer never lets himself down with his body language. He never lets the state of the course, or the quality of the opposition, determine his body movements. He *owns* his body controller. And when a golfer takes responsibility for his body he allows himself to take ownership of his performance script. In turn he plays Golf Tough. This state of mind and state of being gives him the best chance to shoot the score he feels he deserves.

9

Your Second Controller

It was when she passed the 1,000 year old Tower of London that her inner voice started to drive her on. History may have been by her side but it was also in front of her.

"This is just a half-hour run now, I can do this," she had whispered to herself.

And so she kicked on – her inner voice accompanying her stride.

There were swathes of people lining the streets to cheer her every step. They were enjoying the English runner leading her home marathon, but they probably didn't realise they were witnessing one of the greatest performances in athletic history.

....

He crouched on the canvas. His face contorted in agony, the wind knocked out of him by a brutal jab to the solar plexus.

The pain that surged through his body sent his brain into overdrive. Thoughts churned out in quick succession – the referee's count, the world title, the pain, how to return to his feet, his daughter, his brother.

It was his late brother who focused his mind. He chose to dwell on *that* face for a few seconds. He chose to dwell on the feature that would clear his mind and repair his aching body. Then he started to rise.

....

As her feet continued to stretch the pace so her inner voice remained constant and steady. She drove back feelings of pain and stomach cramps by directing her focus onto neutral stimuli – she counted to 100 again and again. As numbers drifted in and out of her consciousness she was able to maintain the feel for her pace as the metres, the yards, and the streets flashed by. With an iron will she preserved her unrelenting speed, running the 24th mile in 5.03 minutes and the 25th in 5.08 minutes. She would cover the last 800 metres in a mere 2.25 minutes.

....

He had taken control of himself. He had shifted his thoughts onto that which inspired and motivated him.

"Suddenly I thought: 'I'm not going out like this, I've got to get up.' I wanted to dedicate the fight to my brother so badly. I wanted to secure the future for my daughter. So I made it to my feet with a second to spare."

He rose and continued to advance. Much to the shock and dismay of his opponent - the IBF Middleweight champion - he was a boxer who wasn't done. With his brother in sight he started to claw his way back into the fight one punch at a time.

....

As she crossed the line to win the 2003 London marathon, expert commentators could scarcely believe their eyes. As she staggered under the finishing banner, the clock above her head showed 2:15.25 beating the previous world best for the women's marathon by just under three minutes. An astonishing feat by a woman whose heart was designed for fitness and whose head was tailored for toughness.

Paula Radcliffe, the world's greatest distance runner, the mental gymnast. Despite the soreness vying for her complete attention throughout the race, she kept a body wracked with ache and hurt functioning to its maximum capacity. For the thousands of hours of training to weave their magic it took an inner voice focused on numbers – a continuous count to one hundred – to displace the pain and to touch athletic history.

....

As he heard the start of the sentence he once again fell to the canvas – this time in ecstasy rather than agony. "And the new...." were words that caused him to explode in a wave of emotion.

Darren Barker was the new IBF Champion. He was skilful, he had endurance, but mostly he was tough. Behind the toughness lay the inner voice that refused to allow him to lie down after being knocked down. And behind the toughness lay his mind's ability to focus on the two things that would drive him most to get up and fight relentlessly – his daughter, and his brother who had passed away after a car crash in 2006 at the tender age of 19. Thoughts of his brother in those final gruelling rounds saw Darren Barker enter the book of boxing champions –a fulfilment of his dreams.

....

Two champions! A runner and a boxer. Two ordinary people competing in different sports demonstrating the extraordinary by using a controller to influence their performance and determine their destiny.

No matter what the sport - the recipe is always the same. A competitor has two simple but critical controllers. As you discovered in the last chapter, you can manage your performance script by using your body language. You can choose to unveil your body controller at any time before, and during, your round. You can choose to stand tall, to hold a positive stance, to swing with confidence, to breathe deeply and to walk in a manner that befits you as a competitive golfer. You can choose to march the fairway at a quick pace – a pace to ignite the adrenaline that focuses your mind and helps you compete at a high unrelenting intensity. Or you can choose to slow your walk rate if your preferred game face requires a chilled, relaxed and calm mindset. You can choose to swing in a leisurely manner or you can choose to rip through the ball with force and speed.

You can act your way around the course – act confidently to become confident, act focused to become focused, and act with belief to feel full of belief. Your body language dials in to instant self-management. But you can double the dosage of control your game deserves. We will now explore controller number two.

Your Self-Talk

Your second controller is the voice you carry with you as you compete. It's that inner speech that never leaves your side. It's your self-talk.

If you want to play at your best under pressure – use your self-talk. If you want to release the club through impact with complete freedom – use your self-talk. If you want to build confidence for that testing five foot putt – use your self-talk. If you want to get 'up for it' – use your self-talk. If you want to calm yourself – use your self-talk.

Your self-talk is a series of words, sentences and phrases that remain private to you, but which guide you through your everyday life. It's that inner voice that sends you left or right. It's the one that tells you to stop or to go. It's that dialogue that works somewhere between thinking and doing and helps you act on the decisions you mentally make. Your self-talk controller is the perfect accompaniment to your body controller – together they are a powerful antidote to inner turmoil and outer failure.

A famous psychologist once said, "Stop listening to yourself and start talking to yourself." This is an important sentence that should permeate the global golfing community. Rather than being a slave to the errant thoughts that can destroy your focus and your confidence - the ones that can fire doubt through your mind and body - ensure that you answer all destructive thoughts with strong, upbeat and confident self-talk.

Self-talk can supply you with inner belief. You can use it to remind yourself of the swings that have hit the sublime shots you've made in your golfing career, as well as the strokes that have squeezed in those 40 footers. It can charge up your focus. You can use it to give yourself a pep talk when it's needed most. When you're distracted you can remind yourself of the task at hand and the swing thoughts that will engage the right part of your body. You can use it to energise yourself. You can pick yourself up after a double bogey or a hole lost. You can urge yourself to remain upbeat despite a lost ball or a shot that's just made a splash.

When I work with soccer players I help them use self-talk to work harder through the last lung-busting 10 minutes. Athletes will use their inner voice to drive them on through pain, through wind and cold, and rain and heat. Baseball players will demand better from themselves if they throw wayward or strike out. Boxers will whisper strategic reminders to their bodies – the ones they need to use as their fight plays out. Tennis players will scream with delight as they win a point that may have seemed lost during an endless rally – but they will also quietly remind themselves to stay cool and calm as the match progresses.

Your inner voice is a guide for your outer world. Keep it confident and focused on what you want.

Your Script's Self-Talk

You may not be able to drive like Rory, rip the stick out like Tiger or putt like Phil, but you can speak to yourself like they do. You *do* have that capability and you *can* have that commonality with the champions of the game. And you already have the perfect platform for inner excellence. It's your performance script and it's ready to go.

You have a game face – the plays you've chosen that represent the very best of you. I'd like you to write them down on a small piece of paper and fold them neatly into your yardage book or scorecard. This will give you the opportunity to refresh your memory of their presence time and time again. Use your self-talk controller to do this. Repeat them to yourself during some quiet time on the first tee. Reinforce them walking down the first fairway. Used as verbal cues throughout the round, they can alleviate a bad start, help you push on following a confident opening stretch of holes, and deliver a Golf Tough performance.

"Stay tall and confident no matter what today. I must remind myself of this after every hole."

"Remember the plays in my game face – it's all about being relaxed. Stay calm and patient... avoid getting uptight and enjoy the round"

"Keep upbeat on the back nine. Be relentless with upbeat – when I walk quick, I feel good and play well. Upbeat and quick at all times."

Self-talk is incredibly effective in keeping your mind focused on your game face and executing the plays that lie within it. It is also useful in helping you complete your brain's routine.

Your self-talk controller can help you to direct your brain's focus and increase your levels of certainty. This is primarily accomplished by holding onto the questioning process I introduced you to in the chapter that outlined your brain's routine. Asking a good question is a component of self-talk – one that engages your concentration and lights up the internal images that float through your mind as you compete. Let's explore some questions that underpin a champion's self-talk:

- *"What does an incredible shot look like here?"*
- *"What does a ripped shot feel like here?"*

- *"What shot will get me closest to the flag?"*
- *"What does a great strike feel like?"*
- *"What would Tiger do here?"*
- *"What is the conservative play?"*
- *"Now I've hit it here, what is the safest route to the green?"*

Questions help you become the director of your inner narrative. Rather than being a slave to your thoughts, you get to influence your pattern of thinking. Just as the clubhead tells the ball what to do, so your self-talk directs your brain through every shot, through every motion, and through every action you take. Provide it with a question and your brain will scan the environment and the understanding it has about your game for the answers.

And you can use your self-talk in other ways during your routine. Cue words can help focus your mind and ready you for the shot at hand. Just by muttering the word "Focus" to yourself you can engage the PFC and fuel your attention control. By whispering the word "Commit" to yourself you can prepare to take a swing that is full of commitment – one that rips through the ball without fear, without tension or anxiety.

I like the players I work with to load up their routine with words that inspire confidence and drive feelings of inner security over the ball.

- *Behind the ball - "What does a ripped shot look and feel like here?"*
- *Walking to the ball - "Only commit"*
- *Over the ball – "Athletic"*
- *About to swing "Commit"*

By talking your way through your routine you can unleash a catalogue of exciting pictures and send a sensation of unwavering belief through your golfing body. By proactively introducing great words into your mind as you follow each step of your preparation and performance routine you give yourself an improved chance to rifle it straight down the middle, hit it stiff, or hole the putt.

Your self-talk controller should follow you as you walk from tee to fairway to green. Use verbal reminders of your game face to clean your mental palette after every shot. Short, sharp prompts of your plays help you forget a duff shot or a missed putt. "Stay confident, stay focused" and similar mantras should be the beat to which your brain manages the emotion that surges through your body.

Quite often you'll find your best rounds have been accompanied by your most helpful inner conversation.

The Voice of a Champion

Your inner voice helps you dig deep. It enhances focus, builds confidence, alleviates negative emotion and keeps you on track when things are going well.

Make a pledge right now – you are going to keep an inner voice that steers your script from the moment you hit a shot on the first tee to the time you hear that satisfying cup rattle on the 18th green. Use this pledge as your template for excellence.

Do bear in mind that using your self-talk isn't easy. It takes effort to shout back when your game goes awry. A bad shot teases and taunts. It goads a poor response. It releases a surge of adrenaline and cortisol that stresses every sinew. If so, then "calm, relax, focus". Allow words such as these to echo with unrelenting force. Urge yourself to stay in control. Your personal self-talk may be silent to others, but - to you - it should be loud and lively.

Now, let's go and put these controllers together. Let's go play Golf Tough.

10
ANA and the ANTs

I'd like you to mentally leap into the future. Step into your imaginary time machine and project yourself to exactly one-and-a-half hours before you tee off in your next competition…

Welcome to tournament day. You are one hour and 30 minutes away from teeing it up. This is your time to start focusing on your objectives for the day. You know them intimately now – execute your performance script by using your two controllers.

"Today I'm going to execute my performance script to the very best of my ability. I'm going to use my body controller and my self-talk controller from the moment I start warming up.

I'm going to use them to dial into the plays in my game face, my course strategies and my routine. Today I'm going to be relentless with my controllers. I'm going to be non-stop. Today I'm going to act out my game face plays and I'm going to talk my way through my routine brilliantly.

Nothing and no-one is going to take me away from my performance script – nothing and no-one. Today, I'm going to be Golf Tough."

As you step out of your car and walk into the clubhouse I want you to enact your game face. If 'tall and confident' is your driving creed, then I want your body controller switched on and tuning into the kind of body language that a tall and confident golfer should portray. Building mind and body momentum before you grace the tee is imperative – this is how winning is done.

Now head for the practice ground. Have a warm up that includes opportunities to take out your controllers. Affirm, in your mind, what you want to achieve over the course of the round. Remind yourself of

your cue words and trigger phrases. Go through your routine for five to
ten shots. Help your body and mind recognise excellence by
introducing them to the physical and mental steps of your brain's
routine.

Give yourself an extraordinary warm up experience. Don't just beat a
few balls, stretch a little, and have a chat with your playing partners. By
all means do these things, but discretely include some mental
gymnastics as you limber up. Experience a confident walk to the ball.
Rehearse an athletic, solid, set up. Attune your body to the feeling of a
committed swing.

When you're ready to play, head towards the first tee – but do so in the
style of your game face plays. Keep building your momentum of
excellence by continuing to engage your body controller. Remember
what the science says – *be it to become it*. And now I want you to add
your self-talk controller. Give yourself a little reminder as you step
onto the tee – "Stick to my routine."

That's great – you've released a hormonal fix of adrenaline,
testosterone and dopamine. Your attention is starting to narrow and
your body is preparing itself to hit it long and straight. Your mind is
tuning in to the task at hand – a solid routine is all you need to focus on
right now.

Go through your routine. Remember to press your self-talk controller
and ask yourself the right questions and work your cue words. Throw
your body controller into the mix – walk to the ball with confidence
and strive to swing with commitment.

When that ball has streamed away I'd like you to reach for both
controllers. Congratulate yourself on a solid first shot and move off the
tee allowing one of your game face plays to shape your posture and
walk. "Upbeat and confident, upbeat and confident."

Relax! Have a chat with your playing partners. And as you get closer to
your approach shot start to bring out your controllers again – you'll
need them to hit it stiff.

Bag goes to ground. Take yourself behind the ball and fix yourself into
the preparation part of your routine. Ask your questions and make your

decisions. Then progress to your performance routine. At this stage you need to immerse yourself in your two controllers.

Move with confidence, swing with commitment, and speak to yourself about freedom.

When the shot's away use your controllers to deal with the outcome instantly. That's what great players do. That's what this week's winner is going to do. That's what next week's champion is going to do. That's what this year's Major winners will do. That's what the leading money winner will accomplish time and time again. 'Getting ready for', and 'dealing with', are the essence of competitive sport.

Combining your Two Controllers

I hope that you're excited at the notion of using your two controllers to take charge of your performance script. Together they are a powerful weapon to think about and act out your performance script. Combined they give you the chance to experience Golf Tough. United they will give you the best chance to produce the result and outcome you want.

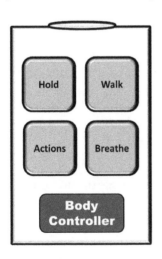

Don't make this process over-complicated. It's really simple. All I require from you, during your next competitive round, is to speak to yourself in the right way and to act and hold yourself in a manner that befits a winning golfer. Rather than trying to win, try to execute your performance script. Rather than trying to make birdies, allow under par scores to take care of themselves by regularly checking in with your game face plays. Rather than trying to break 80 for the first time ever, allow your final score to take care of itself by getting your brain's routine right every single time.

The Golf Tough process of controllers and performance scripts takes care of all outcomes. They take care of winning and top 10's and reduced handicaps and semi finals of knockout tournaments. Dedicating yourself to this process doesn't mean you'll never shoot a bad score again. That's fantasy golf. But what I can guarantee is that if you play my version of Golf Tough you will be the very best you can be on the day. You will shoot as low as your body allows you to for the round you are playing.

But this is far easier said than done. Golf is a difficult game to master, not only because it is humanly impossible to coordinate your muscles with precision on every single shot, but also because your brain just loves to get in your way. The six inches between your ears is full of quirks, idiosyncrasies and oddities. On a whim it can distract you and destroy your confidence. It can stir the wrong type of emotion and it can sap your energy in a heartbeat. Let's now explore a couple of neural peculiarities that can kill your game.

Use your self-talk and your body to manage your swing, your stroke, and your game.

A Brain Called ANA

Your brain is never quiet. It's a cacophony of noise. If you had a chance to take a look at the electrical activity of your brain, it would be like looking down from outer space at electrical storms sprinkling the surface of the earth. The brain is constantly alight, alive and lively. And the result is a never-ending flow of thoughts and images vying for attention in your conscious mind.

This is a process neuroscientists call Ambient Neural Activity, or ANA for short. I'm regularly asked by clients why it is so difficult to turn off the inner narrative that can so often distract. It's because the connections in your brain are constantly connecting, processing and reconnecting. They do so without break or interruption as you go about your everyday life.

This is one of the reasons why concentration in sport is such a challenge. You can be walking down the fairway and all manner of thoughts can invade your mind. Equally you can be going through your routine and unwanted thoughts can enter your conscious mind in an instant. Perhaps you've noticed how thoughts can lay siege to your swing. You may rotate to the top of your swing, with your mind perfectly on task, only to have a thought pop in as you start your descent back to the ball. This is because of ANA. It is the way your brain is designed and it is the way it works. Nothing will ever change that.

You have to deal with ANA. You have to manage the brain's impulse to throw unwanted thoughts into your game. But before I teach you how, let me introduce you to another insidious and destructive feature of your brain.

The brain is designed to distract. It's designed to get in the way – to be anti-Zone!

ANTs

I have ANTs. You have ANTs. The best sports competitors in the world quite often suffer from an infestation of ANTs.

ANTs creep into our mindset when we tee it up on a tough hole. They crawl into our minds as we land in the water or the bunker or the trees. They enter our conscious awareness when we face a tough looking 5 footer for par. Sometimes they appear as we stroll down the fairway, even when things are going perfectly well.

ANTs is an acronym for Automatic Negative Thoughts. These thoughts eat away at your focus and sap your confidence. When they linger they tighten your body and steer your clubhead in the wrong direction. They are a common feature of the competitive mindset because, under pressure, the brain loves to work against you. It doesn't like to work rationally, it's just not designed to. It's there to warn you about the danger – about the water hazard or the treacherous slopes on the green. It's evolved to direct your attention towards the trouble on the golf course. And when our focus is captured by the on-course dangers - the ANTs pile up.

"Don't hit it in the water on the left… last time I went in there… I made 7 on the hole… I've been hooking it a bit today so I really do have to be careful… I don't feel too confident for this shot."

One ANT can multiply quickly. A single, small negative statement can reproduce into dozens of self-critical thoughts that prevent you from hitting your shots with coordination, timing, and fluidity. Combined, those thoughts can cause us to play with fear and trepidation. They can cause us to play with too much care or with an indecisive mind. Great golfers must have a squashing process to deal with the ANTs that invade their mind and their game.

Bad thoughts impede great swings. They tighten your muscles and damage your coordination.

The Squashing Process

SPOT

Perhaps the toughest, but most important, stage of squashing ANTs is the opening exchange. To start with you actually have to notice the ANT in the first place. In my experience most golfers lurch from one thought to the next on the course, without ever really paying attention to the type of thoughts they are having.

Psychologists always preach that awareness is the first step in change. I couldn't agree more - it's a real skill to recognize when you get a little negative on the course.

Golfers tend to play on autopilot. Just as they are unaware of the physical habits they portray on the course they are equally oblivious to the mental patterns that underpin every swing they take and stroke they make. A golfer needs to develop the capacity to recognize how he is talking to himself. He needs to notice when he is thinking in a manner that is destructive to his game. Or as I like to say: "*Spot the ANT*".

Squashing starts with SPOTTING. Building awareness of your inner golfing world - as you play - really is a crucial next step towards mastering yourself on the course. Knowing what you are saying to yourself enables you to know when to engage your controllers.

Spotting your ANTs is more difficult than you may think. Largely because, when you set foot on the course, you are there to play golf, not to analyze yourself. Analysis can, and will, get in the way of performance, so I always ask clients to start this process away from the course in the comfort of their armchair.

Have a think now about some of the negative thoughts you have. When do they tend to come into your mind? There is often a pattern to your ANTs. Maybe it's before you tee off or arrive on the first tee? Taking some time to think about when you have ANTs during the game can improve your awareness on the course.

A second step is to improve your awareness in practice rounds and on the driving range. Training is a time to progress your *spotting* ability. Whilst a practice session isn't the same as playing under the pressure a tournament round delivers, it will still provide a fair reflection on when your ANTs tend to happen. A committed golfer will always take a little time, after their practice rounds, to sit down and reflect on the ANTs he experienced during training.

At some point you will have to start improving your *spotting* during a competition itself. This is tough. Go easy on yourself. My advice is to have several in-game review moments – perhaps after nine holes. Ask yourself *"What ANTs have I heard?"* The reality is that you won't SPOT all the ANTs, all the time, straightaway. This is a skill and it will take time to SPOT them all.

STOP

The next stage is to STOP the ANT. SPOT then STOP! In other words your task is to STOP your negative inner voice from taking shape and affecting your swing, your stroke, and your score.

In my experience the quicker a golfer stops negative thoughts the more effective this technique is. When a golfer allows an ANT to linger the more destructive it becomes. One ANT is quickly joined by other ANTs.

"I hate this course...I never play well on it...I've got no chance today."

"This golfer is too strong for me.....I'm going to lose....this is going to be embarrassing."

"This hole is so tight... I've got very little chance of hitting the fairway... I could rack up millions here!"

Stopping ANTs is simple in theory but difficult in practice. All you need to do is see a STOP sign in your mind. It's like seeing a big red STOP sign, the one you see on the side of a road. An alternative is to say STOP to yourself. You can scream it in your mind. STOP! You need something that you can consciously see, or say, that will snap you back into the present moment and instantly stop the ANTs from spreading.

Just as *spotting* requires practice and patience so does *stopping*. Once you feel comfortable spotting ANTs - start to stop them. Do this in practice, on the course, and at the range. The more you practice the better you'll become at taking control of your ANTs.

Stopping an unhelpful thought is as powerful as thinking correctly.

SHIFT

So, you've *spotted* the ANT and you've *stopped* the ANT - now you have to *shift* the ANT. You have to *shift* your negative thoughts to something more helpful and something more constructive.

Now you've become accustomed to spotting and stopping, you need to learn to take complete ownership of your thinking. You do this by using your two controllers, but perhaps most notably your self-talk controller. And you do this by engaging your controllers to direct your attention back to your performance script.

At the heart of shifting is using your self-talk controller to tell yourself to "Forget it" or "Don't worry about it".

*"I've got no chance...(SPOT)...STOP...(SHIFT)... "Forget it"...
"Let's get back to my game face."*

*"I'm 2 down. I feel like I'm going to...(SPOT)...STOP...(SHIFT)...
"Don't worry about it"... "Just execute your routine on this next shot."*

The STOP in the squashing process needs to be followed by self-talk such as "Forget it", "Don't worry about it", "It's not relevant right now", or any other such phrase that starts to switch you back towards your performance script.

This may sound somewhat contrived as you read it, but this is a scientifically proven process that helps sports people win. Beginners can use it and Olympians can immerse themselves in its method. It is a practice that is relevant for any competitor in any sport.

*"That was a terrible shot, I'm playing rubbi... (SPOT)... STOP...
(SHIFT)... "Forget it, the shot's gone". "Be conservative with my strategy on the next and get it back in play."*

"Don't go in the wat...(SPOT)....STOP... (SHIFT)... "Forget the water"... "Get back to my routine, what does a great shot look like here?"

It may appear almost insignificant but this squashing skill (and it really is a skill!) can save you a shot or two per round. It can reduce the emotional baggage the game tends to produce, and it can keep your mind clear and your body feeling confident.

Make it your business to start SPOTTING your ANTs. Employ the ANT STOPPING signal. And engage your controllers to shift your mind away from the ANT onto your performance script. By adding a phrase such as "Forget it" you can rationalize any given situation and turn your attention onto the task at hand.

The Quick and the Dead

People say that golf is a slow sport. I disagree.

Golf is one of the quickest activities on the planet. The ball works its way from stationary to over a hundred miles an hour (in some cases touching 200 miles per hour) in a second or so. Your clubhead does something similar. You place it behind the ball and less than two seconds later it collides with the ball at approaching, or over, a three figure speed.

Golf is raw speed. It's a jab and duck from Floyd Mayweather. It's Sebastien Vettel shifting into sixth gear. It's Usain Bolt once he's into his stride.

And golf doesn't just require this brand of physical speed. It demands mental agility. A sharp mind - a mind ready to switch on, in an instant, is a pre-requisite for superior performance. Golfers may or may not need an athletic body, but they *do* need a nimble, athletic mind.

I want to set you a challenge. I want you to become world class at squashing ANTs. This means spotting them, stopping them, and then shifting them quicker and quicker and quicker. It means going through this squashing process in the time it takes me to snap my finger or clap my hand.

Never, ever let an ANT settle. That's Golf Timid, and I want nothing less than Golf Tough. It may seem unfashionable in the genteel atmosphere of the golf links, but I want you dedicated to raw mental speed.

"I'm playing really bad tod... SPOT... STOP... SHIFT... Forget it... be upbeat, focus on routine, that's all that matters today."

"That was a terr... SPOT... STOP... SHIFT... Forget it... relax, shift to quick walk, last shot gone, now for an incredible routine on my next shot."

In golf you are either quick on the distraction draw, or you are dead. This may sound over the top but this is how I like my clients to see it. I like them to see ANTs as the kind of pest that can play havoc with their game, so much so that they put the skill of squashing them on a pedestal. Taking a no compromise attitude may not stamp out ANTs for good, but you will certainly prevent the kind of infestation that leads to slumps.

Just as a boxer shifts his feet at lightening pace to dodge a punch, so I want you dodging distraction by building the skill of squashing ANTs with speed. The golfer with a quiet mind, free from ANTs, sets his hands and arms and torso free. He can have fun. He can play to win and not to lose. He can play on the front foot and not the back foot. He can play with freedom and not with fear. He can be aggressive when he wants and defensive when he wants. That's a great golfing skill to have.

Driving Your Golf Tough Performance

Chapter Eight

1. Be it to become it – commit to keeping incredible body language.
2. Your body controller has four functions – how you hold yourself, how you walk, your actions and your breathing pattern.
3. Use your body controller to manage your game face plays, your brain's routine, and your course strategies.

Chapter Nine

1. Double your dosage of self-control by engaging your self-talk controller.
2. Use your self-talk controller – stop listening to yourself and start talking to yourself.
3. Use your self-talk controller to ask yourself great questions – this focuses the mind and builds confidence for the task at hand.

Chapter Ten

1. The never-ending internal chatter you experience is a natural brain process called ANA.
2. Manage ANA and its accompanying Automatic Negative Thoughts by SPOTTING, STOPPING, and SHIFTING.
3. Your golf mindset requires speed – squash the ANTs quickly.

11

Progress with Pinpoint Putting

When most people think of Liverpool they tend to think of two iconic names – Liverpool Football Club and The Beatles. Perhaps I'm a little different to the norm, but when I think of Liverpool and the Merseyside area I think of golf.

This may be a personal bias. Liverpool is home to Hillside Golf Club, which is where I teed it up in the final qualifying round of the British Open back in 1998. This was the closest I ever came to playing in the oldest and grandest golf tournament in global golf. Sadly, winds that registered 50 miles an hour inflated my scores somewhat, as did my mindset – I didn't have my controllers out that day I can assure you!

I also think of golf when I think of the Lancashire coastline because there are so many great courses in the area. Hillside is joined by Hoylake, Royal Lytham & St Annes, Royal Birkdale, Fairhaven, Caldy, Hesketh, West Lancs, Formby, and Wallasey. The north-east of England really is a golfer's paradise - a corridor of immaculate windswept Links, some of the most challenging in world golf.

In amongst the greats is a course that is as stern a test as you're going to find. It's a course called Formby Hall and is a Parkland alternative (perhaps antidote even) to the excess of coastal courses that the aptly named 'Golf Coast' has to offer. At over 7,000 yards it's a long course for England, where land in such a small country is at a premium, and it's a tough enough track to have hosted several professional events.

I'm a regular visitor to Formby Hall, but not always to play the golf course, more often to see one of the global experts of the game. His name is Phil Kenyon. And he can help you putt better.

The Putting Lab

I'm standing in Phil's putting lab at Formby Hall and I have three eyes on me. Phil is the owner of two of them and the third belongs to the camera that he has placed between my feet. He's monitoring my stroke, and he's doing so with several eyes for detail.

He's using a specialist computer program to track my technique – one that complements his experience and one that delivers the data to confirm what he can already see. The result is the kind of feedback my game needs. I have a slightly in-to-out stroke leading to an inconsistent strike. I'm not rolling the ball well enough and I'm not starting the ball on the intended target line. Phil has some solutions for me!

As my new putting guru helps me establish a stroke to get the ball rolling end-over-end, I think back to all the putts I've missed. I try to recall the ones that have lipped out, or missed fractionally left and right. I'd like you to do the same thing. How often have you missed the putts you should make? How often has that ball slid past the hole from eight feet, 10 and 20 feet? How often have you three putted from positions where you really should have taken two to get down?

As a young golf professional I always felt that putting was a discipline of feel and mindset. I believed that if I practiced for long enough my hands, arms and shoulders would get to know how far back, and through, my putter needed to go in order to get the right pace. I believed that this kind of philosophy summed up the technical side of putting. And I also supposed that if I saw enough putts tumble into the hole I would radiate with confidence even on the sloppiest of greens.

But from the thousands of hours I spent coaching the game both technically and psychologically, and from discussions with world class putting coaches like Phil, I've learnt that if you want to hole more than your fair share of putts you have to take a slightly more rounded approach to developing your game on the greens.

Phil Kenyon is, in many respects, the ultimate golf putting coach. He was taught by the legendary putting guru Harold Swash who was a family friend and mentor. Harold Swash had set up the original putting school at Formby Hall and it was after several years of guidance that

Phil took the reins. He complemented the practical putting advice given to him by his teacher by undertaking a degree in sport psychology and following this with a Masters degree in Motor Learning and Control. He slowly became the complete putting coach!

Subsequently Phil's advice has been sought by some of the world's best golfers. He was teaching Darren Clarke when the Northern Irishman won the 2010 British Open and he has had long relationships with players such as Lee Westwood, Thomas Bjorn, and Henrik Stenson. So if there was ever a go-to man on the art and science of putting it's Phil. And my work with him enabled me to burst some of those early myths I had espoused.

The best putters have a consistent stroke and a consistent mindset as they stride the greens.

The Myth of Putting

I have read various books and articles that state putting is all in the mind and is technically the easiest part of golf. Some claim that if you can throw a ball with reasonable accuracy then you can putt with precision. They say that putting is as natural as walking. It requires little exactness – just practice and you'll get better.

I can't argue with the notion that any old Joe can purchase a putter and go putt a ball. And Joe may hole a few putts. But if Joe wants to be the very best golfer he can be – if he wants to hole a high percentage of putts from under 12 feet and roll the ball close, from up to 50 feet away, on a consistent basis then he needs to develop a sound, repetitive stroke.

Putting is both a mental *and* technical discipline and fails to fall predominantly on either side. It is an exploration of your ability to develop a technically proficient stroke as well as a study in your ability to hold an iron-willed nerve under pressure. Phil Kenyon, a man who has taught some of the best golfers in the world, agrees.

Phil's education as a coach included sport psychology. He appreciates that, without a sound mindset, golfers competing at any level will never find consistency on the greens. But the best players in the world don't visit him at Formby Hall just to get the latest trick of the mind. They want to improve their strokes. They know that a shot here and a shot there can be gained by improving the motion of their putter head. They want to know that when they release the putter head through the ball - the face of the club meets the ball at the right angle time and time again.

They strive to improve their putting technique because they want to get better – faster!

Putting is your fastest route to shooting lower scores. It's a no brainer!

Get Better... Fast!

Putting is a discipline of precision. It requires pinpoint accuracy. It requires pinpoint control. It's not like driving the ball, or approach play, where there is margin for error. Push a drive and you can still find the fairway. Pull an approach shot and you may still find the green. Push or pull a putt and you'll discover that the ball won't fall into the hole.

I agree that a putting stroke doesn't require the hand-eye coordination that a full shot demands, and in that respect putting is a discipline that is easier to master than its long game counterparts. But putting is burdened by providing golf with its most obvious outcome moment. You miss or you hole. You fail or you succeed. You add two shots to your score or just the one.

"You add two shots to your score or just the one." Please blow this statement up in your mind. Remember it! Golf Tough golfers care greatly about that one shot. Putting is the quickest and easiest way to knock a shot or two from your regular scores.

A golfer with a repetitive putting stroke will succeed more so than the golfer who has an erratic stroke. Return the putter face back to the ball in a consistent manner, at a consistent tempo, and you'll improve your putting statistics considerably.

The impact that an improved putting technique has should make your next step with the flat stick a no-brainer. If you want to break 90 go and get a putting lesson. If you want to beat that 80 barrier go and get a putting lesson. If you want to be consistent in your scoring - head to the pro shop and book in a series of putting lessons. Because everyone has the physical ability to craft a near perfect putting stroke, there isn't any other element in golf that you can improve as quickly as you can with putting.

Developing your putting requires a combination of technical lessons, purposeful practice and an effective mindset. The simple action of engaging in instruction isn't enough. You need to practice intelligently and you need to coat your putting technique in thick layers of mental skills. With those in mind here are my 3 P's for putting excellence.

Purposeful Practice

By taking putting lessons from a PGA professional you will automatically start to employ purposeful practice. Use their technical advice to crank up the focus of your practice. Do so on your club's practice green but also at home. The beauty of putting is that you can work on your stroke indoors with a couple of balls and a mug for a hole.

All too often I see amateur golfers (and some professional ones as well) walk onto the practice putting green, throw two or three balls down, and start stroking the ball mindlessly towards a hole. Just as you discovered in section one of Golf Tough, practice requires protocols that take into account your current strengths and weaknesses, and which primarily improve your putting through skills tests.

Proper practice delivers pinpoint precision on the putting green.

Putting Skills Tests

Phil Kenyon is a putting coach who sets his clients homework. He has devised a range of skills tests that help golfers create a performance environment within their practice sessions because he wants players to create the right playing habits on the practice green. He wants them to practice just as they'd play. So whilst he works hard on the technical aspect of putting, he encourages golfers to limit how much time they spend constructing a repeatable stroke. He sets out a programme of testing that puts their brain and their stroke under pressure.

A simple skills test that Phil has devised is one that assesses technique, focus and one's ability to cope with frustration. It's very challenging!

He measures a one foot radius around a hole (using ball markers) that is on a slope or incline, and then he places tee pegs at various distances from 5 feet through to forty feet. Your task is to stroke as many balls consecutively as you can within the markers. He asks players to log their score then to try and beat their initial attempt.

A similar version of this test is to place tee pegs at five, ten, fifteen, and twenty feet from the hole. Start stroking five balls from the closest distance, and only when you've managed to stroke all five into the one foot circle are you allowed to move back to ten feet. If you fail at any given distance you have to go back to the beginning. This is a great way to learn how to hold your nerve and control your emotions. Envision getting to that final putt, missing, and knowing you have to start again – ouch!

Phil's putting skills tests are just like Hugh Marr's from chapter 2. They exercise the consistency of your putting stroke and your ability to putt under pressure. With a little imagination, developing your own putting skills tests is simple. Putting balls from different angles with a target of consecutive putts held or striving to stroke the ball within a given radius of the hole are useful barometers for measurement. When you engage in your tests, go through your routine every time. Use the processes and methodologies I offer in this chapter.

A prime putting key for Phil is the ability to take your practice putting mentality onto the course with you. Over the years he's seen plenty of golfers who putt incredibly well on the practice green but find it enormously challenging to take their form to the course.

As we discussed in section one, skills tests put you under pressure and build performance confidence. Setting yourself a goal of holing a certain number of putts from three to six feet stresses your brain and nervous system, especially with the final few putts. But when you do achieve your skills test goal you'll get that deserved injection of confidence you can take to the course with you.

Pygmalion Putting

I like golfers to have high expectations of themselves when they play golf. And research from psychology suggests that having such an attitude is important.

The *Pygmalion effect* refers to the phenomenon in which high expectations lead to higher levels of performance. It is akin to a self-fulfilling prophecy – whatever you believe about yourself, and whatever you expect of yourself, so your performance will closely match these sets of expectations and beliefs. This psychological experience was named after the George Bernard Shaw book and immortalised in the film *My Fair Lady*, in which a girl from a lowly background is taught how to behave in high society. And research by a psychologist called Robert Rosenthal demonstrated the Pygmalion effect in the classroom. He showed that the higher the expectations teachers have of their pupils, the better their pupils perform.

Great sports competitors expect great things from themselves. I'd like you to expect great things from yourself. Expect yourself to be a great putter. Expect to putt great. This is imperative - if you expect to putt poorly you will no doubt miss time and time again.

However, let me be clear. When I ask you to increase your expectations on the putting green I'm not asking you to expect yourself to hole all putts. I am not asking you to expect yourself to single putt every green. Nor am I asking you to expect yourself to take less than 30 putts a round. That's fantasy golf. These are not reasonable or rational expectations and will serve no advantage with the short stick in your hands.

My definition of great expectations for your putting is a little more subtle but far more powerful. From a mindset perspective great putting is stroking freely through the ball. It is the banishment of fear and doubt, anxiety and worry. It includes no tension or tightness or trepidation. Great putting is simply stroking through the ball with a feeling of complete freedom.

And this is where I want you to place your expectations. *"I expect to putt the ball with freedom. I expect myself to stroke freely through the ball. That is all I can expect of myself and that is all I can ask of myself."*

In Phil Kenyon's experience he sees more putts missed as a result of fear than anything else. He believes the closer one gets to the hole, the more fear tends to grip the average golfer. Under the grip of fear golfers will tend to steer. They will tend towards tightening up and trying to control the putter as it works back and through.

The perfect antidote to this is to have a simple putting philosophy as you play and perform – stroke freely through the ball.

"I expect myself to putt great. Putting great is simple – it is stroking freely through the ball."

Train this feeling of freedom on the practice putting green. If you have 30 minutes to work on your putting spend 10 minutes on technique, 10 minutes on skills testing, and 10 minutes on rehearsing your free stroke through the ball. Utilise your body controller on every putt – experience the sensation of your hands, arms and shoulders working in tandem with freedom, as the putter blade works back and through. It is this feeling of freedom aligned with great expectations that provides a platform for consistency on the greens.

I like my clients to utilise their two controllers as they walk onto the putting surface. I like them to exercise their body language and self-talk as they go through their routine. I like them to be process oriented.

Expect to putt well – but make sure
you define what good putting is first.

Process Putting

Just as you have a routine for your full swing, so you should have a simple and reliable routine for your putting. And just as I want golfers to define great putting as a free stroke through the ball (and expect themselves to do this), so I want golfers to be immersed in the process of performance as they putt.

To my mind it is vital to place process ahead of outcome. Too many golfers get caught up in outcome. Too many worry about the hole and holing the putt. I see the hole as your source of anxiety- a mind that is directed towards it is one that is easily stressed. I like my clients to remove the hole from their minds. I believe that once you've read the putt you need to direct your focus away from the hole to a specific target. But more on this in a minute, let's begin our routine from the very beginning.

A world class putting mindset starts long before you draw the putter back away from the ball. It begins as you make your final few paces before you set foot on the green. This is the time to take out your body controller.

Stride onto the putting surface as if it's yours. This is your area of belief. You may not be the best ball striker. You may not coordinate your hands, arms and torso like some players can, but the putting green is your home. You are in your element on the greens.

Great putters believe the putting green is their home away from home. They feel more comfortable on the green than anywhere else on the course. And as you discovered in section three of Golf Tough you can use your controllers to create this love for putting. You can employ your two controllers – your self-talk and your body – to immerse yourself in the process of putting excellence.

Walk confidently as you stroll onto the green. Get your self-talk controller out and tell yourself: "Great, I love this part of the game. I'm going to put a free stroke on this and give the ball a great look at the hole." Use your body controller to stand tall and be authoritative with your movements as you mark your ball and step back to allow your playing partners time to putt.

When it's your turn to putt re-mark your ball and start to read the line. Now is the time to pinpoint your focus and emphasise your confidence. Read the putt with a *sense of commitment* and *decisiveness*. Think decisive and *be* decisive. Maintain this sense of strong-mindedness and certainty as you prowl the putt.

From their read some people like to focus on the whole line of the putt whilst others like to pick a small target to aim at. There is no right or wrong way, just make sure you do the same thing every time. And make sure you maintain your feeling of commitment to your chosen line or target.

When you're ready take your stance next to the ball and, just as you do with your full swing, take some practice strokes as a blueprint for the real thing. Incorporate a keyword – belief, free, confident, focused, commit or solid might be a useful self-talk process at this stage.

When you're ready, place the club behind the ball and re-create the blueprint you've just experienced in your practice stroke. Let it go. Enjoy a free but focused stroke back and through the ball on your line or towards your target.

And that is all you can do. That is all you can expect of yourself. Read the putt with confidence and certainty, take some focused free practice strokes and then let it go. You can't force the ball to go in the hole. You can't make great putting happen. You just have to let it happen. There really is nothing else to it.

Nothing More to Do

When I work with clients on their putting a question I often ask is, "Once that ball has left the face is there anything else you can do?" The answer is always a no. Once the ball has gone then it's gone. Let it go. Pick the ball out of the hole or refresh your mindset ready for the next putt.

If you were to go for a session with Phil Kenyon he'd reinforce this impression of putting. Once one putt has gone, the key is to restore and re-engage ready to execute another process-led routine.

This, to me, is the ultimate putting mindset. Take each and every putt as it comes. Avoid the mentality of letting one putt affect another. If you've three putted the previous green because you rammed your first putt eight feet past the hole, stop yourself from tightening or 'lagging up' on the next couple of greens. This form of putting contamination is one of the biggest killers on the greens. Always keep the same mindset and the same routine for every putt.

If you leave a putt a long way short, or you speed it past the hole, use your controllers to retain a sense of confidence as you hole out. If you miss a tricky short one, use your self-talk and body to preserve your free stroke for the remainder of the round.

Pinpoint putting requires hands and arms that remain unshackled and a mind that remains clear and uninhibited. For evidence of this watch the footage of the PGA Tour this weekend. You'll find those who are putting well are high up on the leaderboard. And you'll find that the champion golfer for the week is the one who doesn't steer or guide or try to cajole the ball into the hole. The champion golfer looks comfortable on the greens. The champion golfer has a focused routine. The champion golfer has a free flowing stroke. And the champion golfer for the week has a putting game that gives the ball more chance to fall into the cup – that is all he can expect of himself. That is all you can expect of yourself.

12

The Mindset of Genius George

The ex-champion knew a good 'un when he saw one. His eye was dedicated to talent spotting.

"I am prepared to back George Gray to play H. W. Stevenson upon level terms with ivory balls for £1000 a side..."

The year was 1913 and John Roberts Junior, the elder statesman of English billiards, was keen to see a young prodigy take on a master of the green baize. Ever the showman, Roberts deemed it compelling viewing – a match between H. W. Stevenson, the former world billiards champion, and George Gray, a young Australian who had exploded onto the billiards scene since his arrival in England just three years earlier.

It wasn't a particularly bold move from Roberts. Despite Stevenson's greater experience, George Gray was showing signs of unsurpassed genius. Gray had travelled from his homeland to pursue his dream of playing the English billiards tour at the tender age of 17 and, despite his youth, had blown away just about every player who dared challenge his brilliance.

The British players had initially scoffed at the rumours coming from Australia. The sporting gossip columns had young Gray tagged as the world's best. Few on the English Tour believed the billiard scores that had won Gray extensive headlines. In fact, word spread that the tables 'Down Under' were comforting to the players – the pockets were said to be a little more 'roomy' promoting big breaks and extravagant scores. But when Gray sailed into England they were in for a shock. He didn't just beat them - he destroyed them.

Scoring for Fun

George Gray looked the part. Steely determination hid behind youthful eyes – bright blues that lit up the room. Speed and serenity, his performance mantra, added to his game face. With a cueing action that was described as scientifically perfect, he played billiards with the carefree manner that befitted a champion.

Gray had mastered English billiards – one of the most popular games of the early 20th century, and the forerunner to modern cue sports such as pool and snooker. With only three balls on the table, billiards relied on vision, technique and mindset and Gray possessed them in abundance. Marching to a quick beat, the unyielding Gray potted red after red. With only three ways to score – in-offs, pots, or cannons, with a mix of two and three points gained for each scoring shot, Gray enjoyed building breaks others envied. When players found momentum, the best in the world at the time would regularly post three figure scores. It was the four figure form that so often proved elusive, but not so for Gray. In the few years he toured England he amassed no fewer than 22 breaks over 1000, and his mark of 2,196 points created a jaw dropping world record!

'Crouch, cue, pot; crouch, cue, pot; crouch, cue, pot,' became his efficient but ruthless manner. And the packed billiard halls lapped it up. Crammed galleries seated A-Z could be heard to gasp in wonder as this exciting warrior of the table potted the pressure angles with an ease reserved for a straight shot 'gimme'. So brilliant was Genius George that the greatest athletic trainer of the day, Sam Mussabini, the man who coached the 100 metre runner Harold Abrahams to the gold medal in the 1924 Olympics (as immortalised in the film Chariots of Fire) was moved to comment on the young man's play. Ever the sporting detective, Mussabini applauded Gray's temperament, discipline and focus. He acknowledged his ability to manage his mood irrespective of success or failure:

"When he is playing badly or is the victim of ill-luck... there are no expressions of disgust. When he is unsuccessful he takes what comes his way in excellent spirit. A close observer may sometimes note a slight raising of the eyebrows – expressive more of wonder than anything else – but of annoyance there is none. If he makes a thousand

break and the packed house shouts in a frenzy of applause, he steps back and quietly bows his acknowledgements, and in it there is neither arrogance nor nonchalance – just a sincere 'Thank you'."

Gray, a mere teenager, was subjected to pressure on a relentless scale. Every day, for up to four hours, he would play in front of packed galleries. But he dealt with the stress of competition by committing himself to the process of winning. He watched his diet and was disciplined in protecting both his hands and feet - anything labour intensive was out of the question. His focus was unbending - something the great Sam Mussabini noted himself:

"While he is occupied with a big break, he has eyes and ears for one thing only. Brilliant strokes may come and go and be signalled with delighted applause. George gives the merest little nod of acknowledgment, and bends down to his work. To him there is no crowd – no anything – except a stretch of green cloth and a little red demon which requires all his attention lest he gain the mastery."

George Gray was exceptionally gifted, of that there was no doubt. But there was another dynamic at play. His billiard tough persona was as much nurture as it was nature - the key to which lay in his relentless pursuit in developing his mindset alongside his game.

The Genius of Genius George

It was Harry Gray who gently teased the work ethic into George. Harry, George's father, was a billiard player himself and knew that excellence was sourced through a foundation of practice, practice, and then more practice.

It was George, though, who had the foresight and industry to add mindset into the mix. His practice regime was arduous but it wasn't necessarily the length of his sessions that eventually bore the champion he became. Whilst he trained his cue action he chose to train his mindset. He focused on focusing better. He worked on his temperament. He rehearsed the calm internal state that enabled him to portray an unruffled exterior.

Section 4 | Chapter 12

So much of Genius George's genius lay in his forward thinking approach to getting the very best out of himself. As a child practicing in smoky billiard halls, back in his native Queensland, he used the noise and background commotion to improve his ability to deal with distractions. At first, disturbances from inside the hall damaged his concentration. Initially he would look up from his cue - his gaze on the ball interrupted. But just as he learnt to stay low to enhance the crispness of his cuing action, so he taught himself to stay low to remain focused. His eyes stopped wandering over to the other side of the room. He remained crouched in his 'ready to pot' position. And his gaze stayed firmly fixed on the balls and the task at hand. He wasn't born with a gift for attention – he *made* his mind stay in the moment, every moment.

Likewise, his cool disposition improved as he started to notice the movement of his inner feelings. Miss an easy shot and he felt the sensation of anger surging through his body. Make a positional mistake and he found frustration seeping through every pore. Instinctively, the youthful Gray knew that these mind and body reactions were billiard break killers. An innings of a thousand or more would be insurmountable without the ability to find inner peace as he played. So Gray worked on the interaction between emotion and action.

He laboured to produce the perfect stroke *combined* with a superior mindset. When he missed he made the decision to show just a small response – not towards himself but towards the table. A subtle lean to look over the baize helped to trick his mind into believing the misplaced shot was down to an unfortunate kick rather than a mis-cue. Why would he be angry at himself when the table was at fault? And he refused to allow himself to get carried away by promising play. The sheepish head nod so eloquently described by Sam Mussabini was formed by years of practicing emotional control. The habit of a bow rather than a clenched fist when things were going his way took diligent repetition. Stifling a competitive spirit was difficult for one who so wanted to win.

The competitive education of George Gray saw the interface between mind and body. He developed his technique and he built a tough mindset to boot. These complementary skills can bring out the genius in us all.

Every Second Counts

Whether it's in my role as Lead Psychologist for England Golf or as a consultant to players of all abilities, I'm often asked how a golfer can practice the mental side of the game. My response is simple and I hope a little eye opening.

The psychology of golf is continuous. It never really stops. It happens every second you play and every second you practice. It beats away in the background as you compete and as you take the time to develop your skills.

Just as Genius George figured out, every reaction and every response you experience following a shot counts. You are *always* practicing the mental side of your game. Your inner reply to a swing or a stroke, whether good or bad, becomes habitual. It is up to you to practice your very best thoughts and your very best actions following poor strikes or wayward shots. And it is up to you to practice your mental fist pump following a ripped shot rifled down the stick. The more you take appropriate action the friendlier the mental side of golf will become.

This exhaustive approach to developing mindset should be mirrored throughout your game. The mentality you adopt when you approach your putts and chips and pitches determines how you feel over the ball. The thoughts you experience as you walk your way down the fairway influences the feelings you encounter as you step onto the green. The inner feelings that grip you as you leave one hole behind and as you march to the next mediates your tee shot mentality. Using the controllers I keenly spoke about in the previous section of this book is a mindset must. It is for *you* to take charge of *your* mindset as you compete. Just like Genius George, it is for you to strive to feel the positive effects of full control.

And this approach shouldn't be the reserve of the golf course. Your mentality away from the lights of the competitive arena is of equal importance. Your mental approach off the course counts as well.

You are always practicing psychology – every thought counts and every feeling matters.

Your 'Story'

A golfer's inner voice doesn't suddenly stop when he leaves the club. Your golf game travels with you. It heads home with you after a round of golf. The brain spends time evaluating your performance. It revisits the key moments – the shots dropped and the putts holed. It replays the good swings and the thinned chips. It reruns the front and back nine, the comments from your playing partners, the unfair bounces and the fortunate kicks.

Appraisal is at its loudest immediately after a game or just prior to teeing off. You compare a round just played to previous outings. You make value judgements on the state of your golf the day before a medal. You estimate your chances of lowering your handicap or winning a big cheque over the course of the next month as your brain evokes the plays you've made in the past few rounds.

This inner dialogue is what I call your 'story'. A goal of mine in any working relationship with a golfer is to help that player manage their golfing 'story'. Essentially, I try to help them manage how they think about their game and how they think about *the* game. An unmanaged 'story' will narrow a golfer's learning experiences and slow down his improvement. A golfer without a firm grasp on his 'story' will suffer from the emotional rollercoaster ride that golf can inject into one's life. He may tend towards being excited about golf one day, and despondent about the game the next. An unmanaged 'story' prevents Golf Tough. How can you play with confidence and focus in the Saturday medal when your practice time throughout the week is impinged with thoughts of failure and shadowed by a 'can't do' attitude? How can you swing with commitment and belief if the 'story' you house in your mind narrates a tale of missed putts, sliced drives, and bunkered approach shots?

It is imperative that your golf 'story', your inner dialogue about your game, is directed in a manner that helps you get the most from your ability. Whatever talent you have, whatever natural affinity for the game you possess, you can only realise your true capability if you exercise your ability to take control of the thoughts you have about your golf. My challenge to you is to engage in several of the mind management exercises I have laid out in this book. Here are some new ones and some that have been mentioned previously. I'd like you to use them to start shaping your own 'story'.

Your inner dialogue shapes your golfing progress. It influences how quickly you develop your skills and how ready you are to play.

Managing your 'Story' = Asking Post Round Questions

Whether it's been an outstanding round or a game to forget, as a Golf Tough competitor you need to take a little time to analyse your round. As we explored in the first section, a part of this process is to record your statistics. The most effective way to sort the good from the bad is to document the objective evidence a round of golf leaves behind.

However, the best players also enjoy keeping a subjective record of play alongside its objective counterpart. Writing some brief notes to complement the stats you collect is a useful way to monitor your mindset and your game. To bring this process alive I ask my clients to refer to three questions after every round of golf they play.

- *What went well today?*
- *What needs to go better next time?*
- *What should I work on to make sure I do better?*

These questions enable you to magnify your strengths, delve into your weaknesses and build clarity by highlighting the areas that will help you keep moving forward.

Communicating with yourself like this helps you to draw a line under a round. Rather than spending the rest of the week dwelling on what might have been, keeping notes on success and failure brings with it the closure that is needed to move onto the next competition with a tidy mind. And it's easier to strike a voice of optimism when you have mentally cleared the dirt of the last round as well as highlighted the best of your previous performance.

If you don't have the time to write down the answers, at the very least make a mental note. If you have the time, and the inclination, getting your thoughts out of your brain onto half a page is ideal. They will serve as memory prompts for future Golf Tough rounds.

Great questions so often lead to a clarity of thought and mind ready to play great golf.

Managing your 'Story' = Rehearsing Your Performance Script

The script you developed when you laid yourself bare in the preparation section of Golf Tough is your ideal template for thinking like a champion.

Your game face, course strategies, and your brain's routine are in-play processes that should be acted upon on the course and thought about away from the links. I strongly advise you build the main thread of your 'story' around them.

"I stick to my game face no matter what. I execute my chosen course strategies from the first tee to the eighteenth hole approach shot. I never relinquish my brain's routine. There isn't a course, an opponent, or a condition of play that takes me away from my performance script. This is the golfer I am."

If you fail to break your handicap, or you miss a cut you should have made, take time to shape your golf 'story' for the week by re-affirming your intention to execute your script better next time. The golfer who has shot over his handicap should strive to re-acquaint himself with his game face plays. The golfer who has lost should commit to a 'story' filled with thoughts of the successful completion of his brain's routine.

"Next time, nothing and no-one will take me away from my performance script."

Produce a 'story' rich in Golf Tough words, sentences and phrases. Load your narrative with Golf Tough actions, attitudes and behaviours. That is what champions do.

Managing your 'Story' = Squashing ANTs

I introduced you to the concept of ANTs in the previous section. But their presence isn't reserved for the course. In fact, it is during your downtime off the course when they tend to infest your mind.

Just as I advised you to do in competition, I'd like you to become skilful at squashing ANTs when they sneak into your mind away from the course. Allowing them to take a hold, to build a nest, damages your ability to enhance your skill level during your practice sessions and stops you from building the momentum of confidence that pressure golf requires.

When an ANT pops into your mind - spot it, then stop it, then shift it, just like I taught you to do on the course. There is no difference in this process. Spot 'em quick and stop 'em quick – the more they take hold the greater chance they have of affecting how you feel about your game. Shift them by guiding your mind back towards what you are trying to accomplish in your game. Shift them by directing your attention towards the plays in your game face or your brain's routine. Shift them by recalling your best games or your best golfing moments. Shift them by developing a can-do 'story'. For as long as you remain in 'can't mode' then you simply won't be able to.

SPOT STOP SHIFT your ANTs with speed off the course as well as on it. Letting ANTs multiply in practice will sap your confidence on the first tee.

Managing your 'Story' = Learning the Mental TAPP Dance

Golf is a game where trouble is always close by. I'm not just talking about the hazards that await you on the course – I'm referring to the bigger picture of developing your game and playing to the best of your ability week in, week out.

Section 4 | Chapter 12

All golfers are subject to poor rounds and periods when posting a good score may feel unlikely. Those who dedicate themselves to improving their swing will likely experience a time when the alien feelings of a new movement overwhelm them. They take to the range optimistic that they can groove their technique, only to leave an hour later desperately disappointed with the outcomes they've seen. Building skill in golf is as much down to will and tolerance as it is anything else.

Golf is a game of peaks, troughs, and plateau. It cannot be perfected and when you feel you've got it mastered it bites back with such severity that many put their clubs away for good.

As a sport psychologist I find many of the conversations I have with golfers involve the challenges outlined above. It is the emotional rollercoaster ride that can make golf addictive, but also a game people love to hate. The good times inject an air of optimism into your 'story' while the bad times convey an overwhelming sense of pessimism. Your 'story' can be hit hard by the troughs.

Over the past 10 years I've found that four words, when combined, have made the most impact while trying to help players soothe frustration and temper doubt. I have noticed myself repeating these words so much that I have joined them together to create a useful, catchy and easy-to-remember acronym for clients to store in their mind.

I ask all of my clients to TAPP. The T stands for Trust, the A for Accept, the first P for Patient and the final P for Practice. I find players deal with the ups and downs of golf better when they commit to this mental TAPP.

When things aren't at their best on the golf course, whether you've just shot well over your handicap, or if you're failing to ingrain the technique your coach wants you to incorporate into your swing, I'd like you to TAPP. *Trust* your ability, *Accept* that golf delivers tough times, remain *Patient*, and direct your focus onto the best possible *Practice* sessions that you can execute. Your practice sessions over the long term will see you lower your scores and groove a swing and a game you can be proud of.

Trust, acceptance, patience and practice are four words that you should deliberately and purposefully include in your 'story' on a daily basis.

They help clear your mind when it's fogged by worry and doubt by introducing the rational perspectives of *trust* and *patience*. If you *trust* your ability and stay *patient* then, in time, you will reach your destination. Simply by *accepting* that improvement in golf can be elusive you temper your concerns over a lack of progress. And directing your brain toward the *practice* ground is the ideal way to mentally cope with a bad round. Commit to the practice protocols I outlined in section one and those great scores will soon materialise.

Trust your ability. Accept the challenges the game brings. Stay patient. Direct your focus onto your practice sessions.

The Silent Assassin

Genius George Gray beat H. W. Stevenson twice in three games. His skill and his will had conquered the very best the game of billiards had to offer.

Just like Genius George did, make the mental side of your game your silent assassin. The great thing is that nobody else needs to know. Whilst others are putting beach balls between their legs to coil more effectively, and others still are putting towels around their torso to help them connect their body with their arms, you can quietly and nonchalantly develop your golfing mindset. People are ready to do all kinds of funky things to get better – I'm simply asking you to improve your thinking whenever golf passes through your mind!

You can do this anywhere at any time. You can establish your play book of powerful golfing pictures while you have some down time at work. While you brush your teeth you can sharpen the golf images housed in your mind. You can choose to shine a light on your very best golf, your best swings and your best putts at any time during your day while at home, at school or college, or whilst at work.

Learn to catch the 'story' that kills your confidence. Spot it and stop it and shift it. Remove the cloud of pessimism by directing your inner voice to your script – the three processes that will help you take on any opposition, punish the course, and shoot the lights out.

13
The Secret of Negative Thinking

24 miles above the Eastern plains of New Mexico an Austrian daredevil stood with the world beneath his feet.

Thousands of hours of training had come down to this one moment of solitary will and the European base jumper was alone in his capsule pondering only two outcomes – death or success. Practice made the latter more likely but the former held a set of inner pictures that were gnawing at his nervous system, and he was having to manage his thoughts to cope with the enormity of what lay ahead of him.

He was attempting a jump from the edge of space. He was trying to do higher and to be faster. He wanted to plummet to earth at the speed of sound – the first human to do so without vehicular power. And he wanted to do so from a height that touched the darkness of outer space.

His capsule had opened at 128,100 feet with 24 miles of cold blackness below him. As he crept closer to the edge of his capsule he edged closer to history and to the destiny he had been dreaming about since he was a small boy. But it wasn't the altitude that worried Felix Baumgartner. The height he could handle. His mind was calm when he thought of the distance between himself and the land beneath him. It was his space suit that was causing the mental leak. A man built for freedom, quick reaction and flexibility - the bulging space suit was not only physically prohibitive but it also engendered a claustrophobia that dulled his senses and slowed his awareness.

In the lead up to the world record sky diving attempt his mind was constantly awash with fear. All the skill he had learnt whilst base jumping and sky diving around the world was rendered redundant in his space suit. He was wearing big gloves and the movement in his neck was prohibited. Less a second skin and more a heavy laden cloak, Felix had to overcome the nagging doubts that were eating away at his confidence.

He had even stepped away from the project for a brief period. But after seeing his replacement adorn the space suit in training, and seeing the reserve man's name in lights, Felix had forced himself to step back into the hot seat. Fear was preventing him from the excellence required to complete the mission but what drove him back to the project was another fear - a fear of failing - a fear of allowing his dream to slip by.

Back in the project Felix had to overcome the destructive thoughts he had of his space suit. In his words he had a "train of negative thoughts" that had to be stopped and crushed. Every time he drove to Lancaster, California, where the test base was, his negative thought train took power and accelerated. His thoughts directed him to the restrictiveness of the spacesuit, the image of which aggravated his confidence and damaged his focus before a day of testing. But over time he learnt to gently shift and nudge his thoughts towards a more productive place. Eventually, whenever he thought of the space suit his mind settled on more confident pictures.

It was this period that taught him how to manage his mind. And this skill became a life saver once he stepped out of the capsule and plummeted back down to earth. As he fell through earth's atmosphere at an enormous speed he started to spin. He considered pushing the button that released the drogue shoot – it would stop the spin but his attempt at world record speed would be over. This is when his 25 years of experience and his new found ability to manage his mindset kicked in. He remained cool. His intense focus was driven by fear – he didn't fear dying, he feared the failure of going supersonic. So he collected himself and managed to get his freefalling body under control. The rest took care of itself and when he opened his parachute he fell to earth gracefully.

People call Felix Baumgartner, Fearless Felix, but the reality is different. Fearless Felix has never really existed. It was fear that held him back and it was fear that drove him. And it was managed fear that helped him conquer the challenges he faced before he went up in his capsule and as he fell through earth's atmosphere.

At his moment of destiny on 12th October 2012, some 24 miles above the surface of the earth he announced to the world "I'm going home now". And then he jumped. He did so with a clear mind. He did so with focus and confidence. He was thinking like a champion.

Thinking like a Champion

Until his jump from the edge of space Felix Baumgartner may never have considered speaking with a sport psychologist. But as the reality of what he was trying to achieve sank in, and as his body reacted to the pressure in ways he had never experienced before, he decided that a little extra help was needed on the mental side of his preparation.

Quite often, sports competitors feel compelled to tell me that they are brilliant at thinking positively. Maybe they are, but I guess any statement made about positive thinking - in my presence - stems from a belief that sport psychology is about 'being positive'.

The belief that I or my fellow sport psychologists are 'positive thinking gurus' is neither flattering nor correct. In fact, it's plain false, and science is starting to support the idea that being successful in any walk of life requires a much more complex form of thinking.

Fear and doubt and worry would never be included in a category of positive emotions, yet it is so often these types of feelings that lead us to take appropriate action. If Fearless Felix hadn't experienced fear he wouldn't have spent the thousands of hours planning, checking, and re-checking his equipment and his safety procedures. Similarly, if Baumgartner had condensed his thinking to the positive he wouldn't have recognised the mental challenges he was facing. He wouldn't have sought expert advice in this area. He wouldn't have found solutions for the internal battle he faced.

Sporting champions lift the trophy, win man-of-the-match, or have the gold medal placed around their neck, not because they experience a never-ending swirl of positive thinking, but because they lean towards thinking effectively and thinking helpfully. There is a difference and it matters to your golf. To illustrate, let me introduce you to a present day sporting idol.

Sport psychology offers so much more than positive thinking pseudo-science. Great thinking is a complex process.

The Psychology of a Champion

Many say he is the greatest Olympian ever.

It's no surprise. A typical training day in the diary of the 'Baltimore Bullet' was oriented to being the best. Get up at 6am. Swim for a couple of hours followed by gym. Something to eat, a sleep, then more working out. Day in, day out, he committed himself to this programme.

A structure for a champion, maybe, but according to his long term coach it wasn't his rigorous training programme that set him apart from his peers. Nor was it his immense physique, the incredible support he garnered from his family or the club he trained at that was known for producing elite level swimmers. All those played a part but it was another component of performance that his mentor believed helped him win more gold medals than anyone else. According to swimming coach Bob Bowman, it was his psychology and his mindset.

From the age of 12, the Olympic swimmer, Michael Phelps, trained his mind. With the help of Bowman he exercised his confidence, his powers of focus, and his ability to imagine every day - before, during, and after his swimming practice.

Bowman instructed Phelps on visualisation. He asked him to watch his 'personal videotape' before he went to sleep and just after he woke up. Of course this wasn't a real tape – it was an imagined movie formed in the mind of Phelps, one that helped him create a blueprint of success. Bowman had this to say about his then young charge:

"He's the best I've ever seen, and maybe the best ever in terms of visualisation. He will see it exactly - the perfect race. He will see it like he's sitting in the stands and he will see it like he's in the water."

But it wasn't just success that Phelps pictured. Bowman continues:

"He also spent time picturing things going wrong. The worst case scenarios."

Phelps would visualise his suit rip or his goggles fill with water.

"He would then have this picture in his database. He would have a set of solutions just in case a problem would arise during a swim meet. His nervous system would know what to do – it would be ready and prepared. He'll pick the one that is most suitable should he need to."

Such an approach may appear negative. Why would Phelps want to think about things going wrong or messing up before a swim meet? Well, before you judge this thinking approach, let me tell you a little story as to how this exercise helped Phelps win one of his many gold medals.

A Tale from Beijing

He knew there was a problem as soon as he hit the water. It was the Olympic Games in Beijing and this could have been a disastrous moment for him.

And after just a few metres the exact challenge he faced became apparent. Not only did he have a race to win against the finest swimmers in the world, he also had water leaking into his goggles.

It wasn't much at first but, as the lengths passed, so more water saturated the inside of the protectors that were supposed to shield his eyes from the water. He couldn't see! He couldn't see below him or in front of him. He didn't know where he was in the race – his location nor his position.

But he didn't panic.

He didn't panic because he'd been in this position before. Not literally of course, but mentally. He had spent many years planning for this eventuality. He had rehearsed it time and time again in the quiet of his bedroom – in the quiet of his mind.

As he turned into his last lap he calculated how many strokes his arms had to pump. It would be 20, maybe 21. He then started to count. His body remained perfect in its technique. He was relaxed but functioning at a high level of intensity. He soared through the water while he swam at full strength.

He could hear but he couldn't see. He could hear the roar from the crowd, but he was blind. They were urging him on but he had no idea he was the recipient of their encouragement.

As he neared the finish line he stretched out for one last surge, a final push. It was enough! He touched the wall before his rivals and as he removed the offending goggles, although his eyes stung from the water, he managed to glimpse the scoreboard. He was an Olympic Champion with a new world record time.

He was asked afterwards what it was like to swim blind. His response was simple and eloquent:

"It felt like I imagined it would."

 Your thinking recipe should include a look at the negative. "What can go wrong?" is a question every golfer should ask.

Negative Thinking

Michael Phelps was successful because of his physique, because of his hard work in training, and because he believed in himself. Positive thinking played a part in that process. Using self-talk and visualisation in a positive way and demonstrating positive body language were important components of his psychological make-up. But integral to his preparation was his ability to spend time in the negative. He understood that 'stuff happens' and not all that 'stuff' will be good - bad luck and an opposition that competes hard and fast is endemic in the sporting arena. A multitude of things outside his control could go wrong (and as illustrated in the story above, did!)

Felix Baumgartner, the greatest skydiver ever, was able to get through his ordeal for a similar reason. It was *effective* thinking and not positive thinking that helped him freefall to glory.

Accepting that tough times are ahead for your golf *must* form a vital part of your golfing mindset. You are not *always* going to shoot great scores. You *will* find some technical changes hard to make. You *will* be subject to the whims of the weather. You *will* be beaten by opposition who are inferior to you and you *will* be annihilated by opposition who are better than you. Your handicap may plateau or go up. Your clubs will feel alien in your hands occasionally. The hole will look minute from time to time. You will get bad bounces and you will fail continuously on some skills tests you set yourself.

Just like life, golf is full of ups and downs and - as part of the process of improving - acknowledging that things can go wrong (and preparing for that) eventually helps you navigate the roadblocks and manage the speed bumps when appropriate. Interestingly, science agrees.

Mental Contrasting

Gabriele Oettingen is a professor at New York University and a global expert on self-regulation, goal setting and goal attainment. She has conducted a lot of research into the effects of thinking about what one wants to achieve. Through this research she discovered that an optimal strategy for setting any type of goal is to take time to think positively about the end goal while thinking realistically about what it will take to accomplish this. She calls this process mental contrasting.

Oettingen certainly didn't have golf in mind when conducting her research but her findings hold true in sport. This is what Michael Phelps was doing when imagining worst case scenarios for his swimming meets. And this is what I help all my golf clients do on a regular basis.

It's not dissimilar to what double gold medallist Michael Johnson did in the build-up to his world record winning runs in the Atlanta Games of 1996. Johnson said that he spent up to half an hour a day visualising his performances – he envisioned success regularly. But Johnson also revealed that he included mental contrasting in his picture book. He would create an image in his mind of getting off to a poor start, having a poor first bend or trailing the leaders down the home straight. He would then strategise in his mind. He would take a little time to think about solutions – to think about being relaxed and clear minded in those situations.

On your journey to becoming the very best golfer you can possibly be you can employ Oettingen's mental contrasting technique. By asking yourself to be realistic about the process of improvement you can self-help and strategise your progress. Here are some questions to ask yourself:

- *I'm not going to feel like writing out my statistics after every round. When is the best time to complete them?*
- *If my skills tests scores are getting worse how should I respond? Do I keep doing them or switch to something else?*
- *When I make changes to my swing how can I get through the times when I hit the ball badly?*
- *If I'm finding it tough to execute the plays in my game face what should I do? What would the world number one do?*
- *My routine will probably break down a few times, per round, due to ANTs and similar distractions. What action should I take when this happens?*
- *I'm sure that some days my controllers will work great, while other days they might be less effective. Should I keep going or should I change something when my controllers fail me?*

You can use mental contrasting on a daily or weekly basis. You can use it prior to practicing, before a lesson, and in the lead-up to a big tournament. Take a few minutes to think about what you want to achieve, then a couple more to picture what success looks and feels like. Follow these inner images with a mental contrasting question. Allow your mind to settle on a solution before moving onto something else.

Using a PGA professional to help you find solutions to mental contrasting questions can be useful. With their experience they can nudge you in the right direction and give you some great ideas on practicing, preparing. and performing.

You don't have to spend ages on this, but the bottom line is that if you take time to think about how you can turn things around when all seems lost, you create a blueprint of resilience that will firm up your mindset under pressure. Building a series of pictures in your mind that paint solutions and 'go to' plans helps you build game toughness and emotional toughness. Do this enough times and your pictures will linger. Eventually they'll stick.

Driving Your Golf Tough Progression

Chapter Eleven

1. Putting is both technical and mental – work on both and see your scores lower, fast!
2. Engage in purposeful practice – this is primarily driven by skills tests.
3. Be a Pygmalion putter and a process putter – great outcomes follow these two crucial P's.

Chapter Twelve

1. Every second counts when it comes to developing your golf mindset – you are always working on your mentality.
2. Your on-course focus and confidence is mediated by your off-course story.
3. Learn the mental TAPP dance – immerse yourself in trust, acceptance, patience, and practice and you'll progress slowly but steadily.

Chapter Thirteen

1. It is effective and helpful thinking as opposed to positive thinking that helps you reach your goals.
2. Accepting that tough times are ahead for your golf *must* form a vital part of your golfing mindset.
3. Use mental contrasting - think positively about the end goal while thinking realistically about what it will take to accomplish this.

14

The 4 P's of Billy Mills

An unknown American stood on the start line of the 1964 10,000 metres Olympic final in Tokyo. His status far from world beater; he crouched alongside the world's best, runners who were frequently posting times that the unknown American had only recently started to match. In fact, only four years previously his very best time for the race that held his destiny was a whopping two minutes slower than the kind of times that won Olympic finals. He faced an impossible task.

Yet the unknown American, full of hard-earned belief from intense daily training sessions, held his nerve and proceeded to run the race of his life. And by the final bend of the last lap he found himself in third place behind only two people – pre- race favourite, the Kiwi, Ron Clarke, and a Tunisian called Muhammad Gammoudi. His presence in the top three during the latter stages of the race was phenomenal. No one had given him a prayer to find the top 10 let alone a medal winning position. But something different was happening that day. His bodily engine was turbocharged – he felt strong, tough, and full of confidence.

As he held his line around the final bend he found he was talking to himself:

"One more try, one more try, one more try."

He was still in third place but he had found a voice to hold his inner strength – one that was helping him maintain momentum through the last lung-busting 200 metres of the race. His physiology was changing moment to moment and his vision was blurred. He felt tingling sensations down his arms and excitement rush through his body. As he hit the home straight his self-talk hardened:

"I can win, I can win, I can win."

Chapter 14

He was now in position to strike, to pounce. Rationally his mind knew he had the world's best in front of him yet he kept reminding himself that he could achieve his goal, he could smash the pre-race expectation. With 30 metres to go he still held third, but his inner voice still had more to deliver:

"I won, I won, I won."

And that's when it happened. That's when Billy Mills, the unknown American pressed his inner accelerator and surged for home. His body pumped testosterone and adrenaline through his system at a rapid rate – his whole physiology ablaze from the hunger to win. He propelled past Ron Clarke and his body thrust itself beyond the exhausted and slowing Gammoudi. And as Mills passed through the finish line, his arms aloft, the usually soft-spoken American commentator, Dick Bank, went, quite frankly, nuts. From high in the stands, set back from the track, he slipped from his calm demure and screamed, "Look at Mills, look at Mills!"

And if you were watching what Dick Bank was watching that day you will have seen the unbelievable. You will have seen Billy Mills win the most unlikely gold medal in Olympic history. The unknown American was in a different place to his competitors. He had exercised his 4 P's every step of the way. He was competing tough and he was running tough.

Minding Mills' P's

Do you dream of better scores? Do you dream of breaking 90 or 80 or going sub- par? Do you dream of reducing your handicap, winning the club championship or setting foot on one of the world's greatest professional tours?

If you desire any of the above, do what Billy Mills did. Commit to the 4 P's of practice, prepare, perform and play. Commit to the processes and procedures that underpin the P's. Trust that excellence lies within them.

Mills is a little known sporting idol, and his accomplishment was a result of finding the rational in the irrational. The depth of his progress in athletics was akin to asking a 12 handicap golfer to reduce his handicap to plus figures then go and compete in (and win) the U.S. or British Amateur Championships. The gulf between Mills and the world's greatest long distance runners just four years before his win in Tokyo was cavernous - he had to find a way to reduce his best time by a whole two minutes.

He started this process by breaking down the enormity of such a gap in ability. Mills logically felt that to run 120 seconds quicker over 10,000 metres would require him to press on his internal accelerator just a little more per lap. Chunking his goal into small pieces like this appeared to him much more achievable. "Just a little more per lap" became his maxim and his training mentality.

You can do this with your golf game. A 15 handicap isn't that far away from single figures if you break down your golf into smaller compartments and look to improve a little at a time in the areas that most need improvement. A small nudge here and a minute shift there, over time, adds up. Be like Mills, be obsessed by the inch and the 1%.

Billy Mills said, many years after winning the Olympic title, that his preparation included visualising the race hundreds of times a day. He would play his inner success movie time and time again. This is the same as the 1% rule of preparation. I want you to engage in some mental rehearsal, for up to 15 minutes a day. By enjoying inner pictures of the plays in your game face - as well as your brain's routine and your course strategies - you create a mental blueprint that will lodge at the forefront of your mind.

When his preparation was complete and he was crouched on the start line, Billy Mills took out his self-talk controller. He spoke to himself with determination, with grit and with confidence as he ran. And on the final lap he tried to delude himself. Whilst in third place he sent a message to his brain "I won, I won, I won" even though he was still in third place! But he knew that this message would send a rush of performance hormones through his nervous system. He knew he would give himself the very best chance to hunt down the two athletes in front of him. He knew his inner voice could take him across that line first.

Do as Billy did. Work your controllers hard as you compete. They are there to help you take control of what you can control on the course. They are there to help you manage your game. Use them to help you swing with confidence. Use them to help you putt with focus. Use them to make great decisions. And use them to help you manage your mindset after the ball has left the clubhead.

Do as Billy did. Be effective with your practice. Be thoroughly prepared to play. Perform with control. And progress with confidence.

Practice, Prepare, Perform and Progress

Commit to world class practice. You don't have to be extraordinary to train with distinction, but too many golfers rely on the ordinary – their practice is wasteful and lacks focus. Be more demanding on yourself than that. By falling in love with the quality of your practice you give your golfing mind and body permission to grow.

Train your golf to the beat of confidence and skill. Find your numbers first then chart your progress alongside your favourite PGA professional – an expert eye by your side will make your journey a little quicker, and a little less painful.

The skill in your hands is not dictated by your technique. It is influenced by your style of swing but it is dominated by your practice environment. Build skills tests into your daily development plan. Practice with a goal in mind and constrict your target as your skill develops. Every champion-elect, no matter their level, should have a stack of cards with different skills tests on them. By putting yourself under pressure in training you create skill wrapped in a thick layer of confidence. You pressure proof your game.

When you do take time to develop your technique - do so with focus. It is concentration that fuses the memory of muscle movement. Take your time. Slowly build roads from pathways, and race tracks from motorways. Exercise patience - the slick sleek technique of the scratch golfer is assembled over years and not months.

Prepare better than others. Broaden the awareness you have of your game by evoking memories of you at your very best. Make those inner images big and bold and bright. Make them exciting and energetic and infused with positive emotion. Physically amplify and mentally intensify each and every game face play in your script. They are your personal templates for golfing excellence.

Know how to get around the course before you enter the golfing arena. Pick your preferred landing spots. Play safe! Great scores aren't made in the trees and aren't engineered from the sand. They are founded on fairway finding shots. Champions plot their way around the course – a process you can adhere to, too – no matter what level your ability. You can choose to think like the best in the world if you really want to.

Develop a repeatable routine that quicksteps your confidence and settles your focus. Make it brain friendly – it's the quirks of the six pounder that will let you down under pressure. Make your routine one that builds certainty as you walk to the ball. Swinging with freedom, with commitment, and with confidence should be your driving creed as your club fires through impact.

A winning mentality is one that binds you to your performance script. Be clear – it is your game face, your brain's routine, and your strategies that create the result, rather than the will for a win. Pledge allegiance to the process and the performance and subsequent outcomes will take care of themselves. Nothing and no one will take you away from your script – nothing and no one.

When you set foot on the course unsheathe your controllers. Control your body and your self-talk to manage your script. Build momentum by displaying your game face plays as you warm up. Talk to yourself confidently. Use your body to show others your confidence and use both controllers to set your inner feelings of excellence – that positive feedback loop will provide the energy and mindset you need to play your very best golf.

Progression in golf is hard. You can have the right systems in place and the right practice structures, but there are no guarantees of improvement. You have to persevere. You have to be patient.

Look to every department of your game for improvement. It will probably start with putting. Everyone has the capability to become a great putter but it is a technical discipline as much as it is a mental exercise. Treat it as such. Show the 'game within the game' some respect and seek professional help to refine your stroke – you'll improve your scores a lot quicker if you do.

Do what Genius George did – work diligently on your mindset. Practicing the mental game is no different to practicing the skills that find the fairways and which hole the putts. It takes time to shape your confidence, focus, and belief.

Golfers who are 'set in their ways' will set their game in concrete. Loosen your footing and have some fun with the process of progress. Enjoy a different, more thorough way of practicing, and engage better performance tools. Most of all, enjoy the new, lower scores that you will post if you adhere, as best you can, to the 4 P's outlined in this book. That, in simple terms, is Golf Tough.

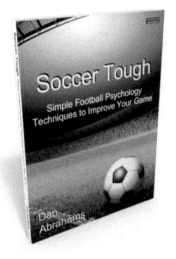

Soccer Tough by Dan Abrahams

"Take a minute to slip into the mind of one of the world's greatest soccer players and imagine a stadium around you. Picture a performance under the lights and mentally play the perfect game."

Technique, speed and tactical execution are crucial components of winning soccer, but it is mental toughness that marks out the very best players – the ability to play when pressure is highest, the opposition is strongest, and fear is greatest. Top players and coaches understand the importance of sport psychology in soccer but how do you actually train your mind to become the best player you can be? Soccer Tough demystifies this crucial side of the game and offers practical techniques that will enable soccer players of all abilities to actively develop focus, energy, and confidence. Soccer Tough will help banish the fear, mistakes, and mental limits that holds players back.

A Round In My Mind: The Golfer and The Sport Psychologist on The Jubilee Course at St. Andrews
by Dr Paul McCarthy and Dr Mark Wilson

In this unique book on golf improvement, follow the fictional account of Chris Marriott, a 4-handicap golfer, as he plays a round of golf on the Jubilee Course at St Andrews – accompanied by a sport psychologist, James MacAndrew.

As each hole presents its challenges, Chris and James discuss their experiences of golf and Chris begins to understand what is holding him back from shooting lower scores and, equally importantly, better enjoying his golf! Written by real-life sport psychologists Paul McCarthy and Mark Wilson, the book covers themes such as emotional control, decision-making, ego versus ability, removing self-imposed limitations, and controlling processes better. By the end of the book, readers will understand how to challenge and address the issues in their golf game that are hindering them. A commitment to change for the better is a commitment that only you can make.

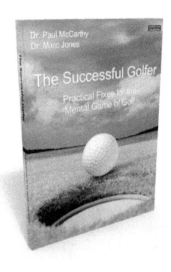

The Successful Golfer by Dr Paul McCarthy and Dr Marc Jones

Written by Dr Paul McCarthy (the first ever resident Sport Psychologist at St. Andrews Links) *The Successful Golfer* is designed to help address 50 of the most common faults that players experience and which hold them back. These include: hitting the self-destruct button when winning, nervousness on the first tee, losing focus off poor drives, and many more. Each fault is remedied with a clear practical fix. Readers will learn to develop effective practice plans, build a dependable pre-shot routine, cope with the pressures of competitive golf, and deal with distractions.

In the second part of the book, lessons from 30 fascinating research studies on putting, practice, choking, and overthinking are presented. In the final part of the book, instructions are provided on developing a number of highly effective techniques that can be used across a wide variety of situations. These include: pre-shot routines, breathing exercises, goal setting, and how best to practice.

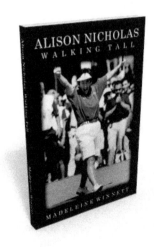

Alison Nicholas: Walking Tall by Madeleine Winnett

Alison Nicholas, MBE, is one of Great Britain's most successful golfers. In a professional career spanning more than 20 years, she claimed 18 tournament wins including the British Open, topped the Ladies European Tour Order of Merit and, in 1997, won the most prestigious championship in golf – the US Open. Her aggregate ten-under-par total was, at the time, the lowest recorded in the history of the championship and led to her becoming The Sunday Times Sportswoman of the Year, and the LET Players' Player of the Year.

In turn, Alison is well known for her Solheim Cup exploits. She played in six, and captained the European team to a famous victory at Killeen Castle in 2011.

Images of the team celebrating in front of the windswept castle have become iconic.

In this candid and entertaining book, Alison explores her years on both the LET and LPGA Tours, the ups and downs, her tournament records, her faith, and – of course – the Solheim Cup. Filled with anecdotes from the other side of the ropes, behind-the-scenes insights, and images from her private photo collection, the book charts the hard work, focus, attitude and good times that led to Alison Nicholas *Walking Tall*.

What Business Can Learn From Sport Psychology by Dr Martin Turner and Dr Jamie Barker

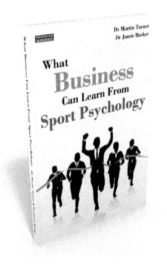

The mental side of performance has always been a crucial component for success – but nowadays coaches, teams, and athletes of all levels and abilities are using sport psychology to help fulfil their potential and serve up success.

It goes without saying that business performance has many parallels with sporting performance. But did you realize that the scientific principles of sport psychology, used by elite athletes the world over, are being used by some of the most successful business professionals? Performance - in any context - is about utilizing and deploying every possible resource to fulfil one's potential.

This book is about getting into a winning state of body and mind for performance – whatever that might be – sales pitches, presentations, leadership, strategic thinking, delivery, and more.

In *What Business Can Learn From Sport Psychology* readers will develop the most important weapon needed to succeed in business: their mental approach to performance. This book reveals the secrets of the winning mind by exploring the strategies and techniques used by the most successful athletes and professionals on the planet. Based on decades of scientific research, the authors' professional experiences, and the experiences of winning athletes and business professionals, this book is a practical and evidence-driven resource that will teach readers how to deal with pressure, break through adversity, embrace challenges, project business confidence, and much more.

CPSIA information can be obtained
at www.ICGtesting.com
Printed in the USA
LVHW060314020219
606046LV00017B/262/P